THE SUCCESSFUL CHRISTIAN LIFE
12 ESSENTIAL SCRIPTURES

David Hoffman

Six week study guide included.

Pastor Dave Hoffman may be contacted at:
Foothills Christian Church
350-B Cypress Ave.
El Cajon, CA 92020
(619) 442-7728

Publisher information:
CSN Books
P.O. Box 1450
Pine Valley, CA 91962
Toll Free: 1-800-636-7276
www.csnbooks.com

Printed in the United States of America.

ISBN: 978-1-7969963-2-6
First Edition 2019
Cover Art by Straight Fire Marketing
straightfiremarketing.com

TABLE OF CONTENTS

The Obvious

Your Word is a lamp to my feet and a light to my path.
—Psalm 119:105

As you begin to read this book, you may notice there is something that I am leaving out: There is not a chapter on the importance of regularly reading the Bible. My hope is that this is obvious, that it is clear before we even start that reading God's Word is the foundation of any successful Christian life.

Moses, in giving his last instructions to Joshua, told him that if he obeyed God's Word, he would have success wherever he went (Joshua 1:7).

All the truth about successful Christian living in this book comes from the Bible, and without it, this book couldn't have ever been written.

It is my sincere hope that you would take these 12 scriptures, memorize them, and practice the truth that is revealed in each.

Because He lives,
—David Hoffman

CHAPTER 1

How to Trust God

---

*For the Scripture says, "Whoever believes in Him will
not be disappointed."*

—Romans 10:11

Imagine you and a good friend are sitting in a modest-sized living room chatting while an 8,000 pound African Elephant stands in the corner. Neither of you know why the elephant is there. He doesn't blend in. He makes it crowded, and he smells awful. You and your friend, however, don't say anything about it. You talk about the weather, you ask each other about work, family life, and all of the typical small talk that people tend to gravitate toward. Your eyes go to the large beast. Your friend's eyes go to it as well. Then you continue talking about sports. Nobody mentions the elephant.

There is something sort of insane about the scenario, isn't there? The first thing any person who walks into the room ought to say is, "Can we talk about the elephant?" This idea is where we get the old expression, "The elephant in the room." It's something that everyone is thinking about but no one mentions, to the point of ridiculousness.

Every organization, culture, family, creed, and philosophy tends to have an elephant in the room, and among those considering Christianity, I believe that question is this: "Am I going to regret giving my whole life to God?" Even those on the outside of faith know that following Jesus means we cannot live the same way before and after. Following Jesus means that we have to give up some things, we have to accept some other things, and that we aren't in charge any longer. We are attracted to things/people/lifestyles that we believe will bring us happiness, so is it wise to forgo our own notions and commit to following God's instructions? What if we miss out?

This question is so pervasive, so pressing and important, that even many Christians struggle with it. We know that God promises abundant life, but what if He forgets about us? What if He's holding back the good stuff and gives us an inferior life in exchange? This is the fear to which Romans 10:11 is the cure.   *interesting*

A PERFECT STANDARD

Put another way, the question is, "Can we trust that God's standards line up with reality 100% of the time?" The Book of Amos in the Old Testament has something to say about that:

> *Thus He showed me, and behold, the Lord was standing by a vertical wall with a plumb line in His hand. The Lord said to me, "What do you see, Amos?" And I said, "A plumb line." Then the Lord said, "Behold, I am about to put a plumb line in the midst of My people Israel. I will spare them no longer."*
>
> —Amos 7:7-8

First of all, what's a plumb line? This is a powerful passage, but only if you understand the metaphor. Picture a large, metallic acorn the size of your fist. Then picture that large, metal acorn tied to a long piece of string. That's a plumb line. Held out into empty space, a plumb line gives contractors an accurate vertical line so that they can build walls straight up and down. You don't need to have a lot of experience to know that walls that lean one way or another aren't very strong, and often they fall down, to the ruin of those nearby. A plumb line sets the standard for perfection, and God sets this in our midst.

Plumb lines are used for building, but they can also be used to inspect existing structures. If I stand on top of your roof, drop a plumb line, and at the bottom the weight is hanging a foot away from the wall, I know that it isn't very straight. Eyeballing it, you may not be able to tell the difference, but in the presence of a perfect standard the weakness becomes all too clear.

The nation of Israel, God's chosen people, had strayed from God's commandments in the time of Amos. God told Amos that He was going to measure them against His perfect standard. Israel had forsaken trusting in God's ways and had run to foreign gods and unrighteous living. They had built their lives on pagan, wicked ideals—ideals other than the standards that God gave them in His Word.

Christians can do the same thing. As Jesus said, they can build their lives upon the sand instead of upon the rock. Then, like the old song says, when the "rains came down and the floods came up," the house built on the sand collapsed (Matt. 7). Those who build their houses upon a foundation of solid rock will weather the storm intact.

Not every believer will have the same experience in their faith. Some will be very obedient to God's leading and instruction in their everyday lives; others will struggle to surrender parts of their relationships, finances, or some other area of their lives.

Even though a person confesses Christ and truly believes in His divinity, it is possible for that person to build his life upon other principles—at least in the short term. Everyone has transgressed God's perfect standard, His plumb line (Romans 3:23). Through confession and forgiveness we enter into His family. We are given the gift of the Holy Spirit, eternal life, and justification before God. This is the gospel.

[Handwritten margin note: to read the word & obey it! & the ball is in our court & the movie & God has done all the]

For the Scripture says, "Whoever believes in Him will not be disappointed."

—Romans 10:11

Friends, oftentimes a new believer accepts the gospel with joy, then at some point later on they are confronted with a situation in which they are tempted to rely on their own ideas. "The boss might fire me *if*," "People might not like me *if*," "*If* I follow God's commandments about tithing, how will I afford…" etc. This important scripture reminds us that God is faithful. If we trust in Him, we will never be disappointed.

To demonstrate this fundamental truth, we have to look no further than the Book of Joshua:

Now behold, today I am going the way of all the earth, and you know in all your hearts and in all your souls that not one word of all the good words which the Lord your God spoke concerning you has failed; all have been fulfilled for you, not one of them has failed.

—Joshua 23:14

When Joshua says, "I am going the way of all the earth," he means that he is about to die. In looking back over his long and eventful life, which was often full of trials and challenges, he says unequivocally that all of what God had spoken concerning them had been fulfilled. He did not break His promise (Numbers 23:19). He did not change His mind (Malachi 3:6). When Joshua's years were fulfilled and he was able to look back over the course of his entire life, he saw that God had never let him down.

Romans 10:11 and Joshua 23:14 remind me that if I do it God's way, even if it goes against what everyone else is telling me, I won't be sorry. The government does not know better than God, our culture does not know better than God, and no family member, friend, professor, or celebrity can ever suggest a better course than building your life according to God's plumb line.

4

MARRYING THE RIGHT WOMAN

When I was in my early twenties, I found myself in a conflict between my desires and God's perfect standard. I was infatuated with a particular young woman and had dated her for 2½ years, even discussing marriage. Great as that might sound, my life during our courtship was a mess. I was partying constantly, drinking like a fish, and taking whatever drug I could get my hands on. Six years of living this way took its toll on my body and soul, and I had to regularly see a psychiatrist in order to try and cope with the constant anxiety, fear, and irrational thinking that had resulted. All the psychiatrist could do for me was give me more drugs to sedate me, to calm me down.

Then, one Sunday evening I found myself in church, and I had a life-changing encounter with God. Growing up with a pastor for a father, I knew about Jesus, but He sure didn't have my whole heart at that point. That evening I knew that I needed to give my all to Jesus, and so at the Holy Spirit's prompting, I got up and went down to the altar before the message was even finished. The preacher looked at me strangely and said, "Well, I guess it's time for an altar call."

Getting right with the Lord was such a relief. He took away my dependence on drugs, I was getting my clarity of thought back—and then my girlfriend broke up with me.

I was devastated. I prayed, "God, I thought when I gave you my whole heart things were supposed to work out! Please bring her back! I know You'll bring her back." I prayed about her constantly. I wanted to marry her, and over the next six months as the Lord cleaned my life up, she began to notice a change in me that she liked. She wanted to meet with me, so one day we ended up sitting together in her white Datsun station wagon, parked outside of my apartment, and she told me that she was thinking about getting back together.

I was rejoicing. Little trumpets were sounding victoriously in my mind. I was praising God and trying not to shout with glee. I had been praying for a moment just like this one to happen.

And yet, I knew clearly what she needed to hear from me. She needed to be assured that I could keep all of this religious stuff in proper perspective, that I wouldn't let this Jesus thing take over my life. If I told her that, I was confident that we would get back together and most likely marry.

In that same moment I also knew what the Lord wanted me to tell her. Jesus wanted me to testify to her what He had done in my life during the past six months. I needed to tell her that my priorities had changed and that I had submitted my life to the Lord. The impression was so strong that there was no doubt about what I was supposed to do.

The problem was, I knew that if I obeyed the Lord that I would probably never see her again. It's funny to me how clear all of this was at the time. I saw two paths laid out before me: Trust God or follow my own emotions. Very slowly and deliberately, I gave my testimony to her. She listened without saying a word, and when I was finished we said goodbye and she drove off.

It was overwhelming watching her go. I went into my apartment, sat on the edge of the bed, and began to cry. I didn't see her until 20 years later when she came to visit our church. It was a hard decision at the time, but I've never regretted it for a moment. God had a better plan for me. When I think about my beautiful wife, Mary, our 30 years together, and our three amazing children (and our in-laws, and grandchildren!), I am at a loss for words. How much could I have missed if I had listened to my own way of thinking instead of God's? That young lady in the station wagon was the wrong woman for me in a myriad of ways, but I couldn't see it at the time.

God saw it. Thankfully, by trusting in Him, I received the better reward.

THE ROAD LESS TRAVELED

I reached another significant crossroads in my life at age 28, when my brother Mark and I were attending a denominational seminary in Dubuque, Iowa. Coming from San Diego, California, living in Iowa was shock enough for both of us, but there was a bigger issue. The seminary was extremely liberal in its theology. It seemed that almost daily we found ourselves defending the inerrancy and infallibility of God's Word. Any scripture that didn't agree with contemporary cultural values was reinterpreted to support current philosophical beliefs. The issue of homosexuality was the most obvious example. Mark and I knew that it was only a matter of time before this particular denomination would embrace homosexuality and begin ordaining homosexuals, which in fact has now happened. I often wondered, "Lord, why did You lead my brother and me to this liberal seminary, a place where we feel persecuted almost every day?"

After two years, each seminary student had to do one year of full-time ministry in a church of that denomination before coming back for the final year. The time had come for me to decide between several churches that wanted me to come and serve their congregation.

I put off making a decision for as long as I could, but I could not escape the question, "How can I become a pastor in a denomination that rationalizes God's Word to fit into the culture's shifting value system?" The answer was simple. I could not. This seemed simple enough; I would leave the seminary after the end of the semester. The ramifications then began to set in.

First, many people had supported me financially during the past two years. They gave money expecting me to become a pastor of that particular denomination. Secondly, I knew that if I stayed I would be assigned to a good church with a very good salary, benefits, and a healthy pension. Finally, there was my family to worry about. What about my father who was so proud that both of his sons were following in his footsteps? Nevertheless, we felt that God was leading us to leave this denomination and the security that came with it, to instead venture into the unknown with God as our provision.

I'll never forget the call I got from my mother a few days after we had sent my dad a letter explaining why we were going to leave the seminary. Mom said that we shouldn't move back to San Diego because she was concerned for Dad's health. She was worried that the stress, shame, and embarrassment of us leaving the denomination would cause him physical harm. As it was, he had taken the news hard and wasn't sleeping. She said it would be better if we moved to another city, away from them.

I had lived in San Diego my whole life. It was home. Mark and I saw that following God's leading would have serious repercussions on our relationship with our parents and many people we had grown up with. As my mom was begging me not to come back home, I was reminded of Luke 18:29–30.

> *And He said to them, "Truly I say to you, there is no one who has left house or wife or brothers or parents or children, for the sake of the kingdom of God, who will not receive many times as much at this time and in the age to come, eternal life."*
>
> —Luke 10:29–30

I knew that decision would be costly, but it has paid back a hundredfold. Without a doubt God has given back to me far more than what I thought I had lost. Years later, I got to hear my father tell me that he had been wrong to react the way he did and that he was proud of my decision. Before he died, both he and my mother sat in the front row of our church every Sunday morning.

COUNTING THE COST

The reason I've told these stories from my life is that I know it's not easy to trust God when you can't see around the corner. We would be deluded to try and claim that following God never costs anything. Oftentimes when we make a hard decision that honors God, things get worse for a while. Don't let your faith be shaken. Everything in life is a tradeoff of one form or another, and trusting in God will never, ever lead to buyer's remorse.

> *Again, the kingdom of heaven is like a merchant seeking fine pearls, and upon finding one of great value, he went and sold all that he had and bought it.*
>
> —Matthew 13:45–46

In the above verse, we see a merchant in search of fine pearls. He finds a pearl "of great value" and joyfully sells everything that he owns to buy it. Don't let the significance of this get past you: Merchants are people who buy low and sell high. Having "great value" means that the pearl is worth more than what he paid for it! Even though he mortgaged his house and sold his livestock and pawned his jewelry, he will get it all back and more. Certainly, the merchant with the pearl of great value will not be disappointed when he receives back far more than what he spent, even though he is without his accustomed possessions for a time.

This can be a hard concept for us because we want control. We have trouble trusting in God's valuation in life because we are prideful, and we want to gain without trading anything. Ultimately, many of us are suspicious of God as to whether or not He has our best interests at heart. We worry that the pearl is fake, even though everything within us tells us it is real and valuable.

This is why many Christians live anxious lives devoid of peace. They lay awake at night tossing and turning as they rehearse all of the worst-case scenarios that might happen. I guarantee you that if you are worried about something and losing sleep over it, it's probably an issue you have not yet turned over to God.

When we surrender our situations to God and look to Him for deliverance and provision, there is no longer any reason to be afraid. When we try and "eyeball it," the walls we build will inevitably be crooked. When we use a plumb line, however, we can rest assured that they will turn out straight, even if it looks off to us for a moment. I am not saying that we shouldn't be responsible, but when you come into a conflict between your way and God's way, go with God's way every time.

There is a cost to trusting in God: Giving up control. As Romans 10:11 promises us, however, the cost is abundantly worth it. The result is a peace that cannot be shaken, knowing that the God of the universe is working on our behalf (Isaiah 64:4). I am convinced by Scripture and over 40 years as a Christian that if we trust God's Word, obey what it says, and live one day at a time, we will know success.

> *This book of the law shall not depart from your mouth,*
> *but you shall meditate on it day and night, so that you*
> *may be careful to do according to all that is written in*
> *it; for then you will make your way prosperous, and then*
> *you will have success.*
> —Joshua 1:8

> *So do not worry about tomorrow; for tomorrow will care*
> *for itself. Each day has enough trouble of its own.*
> —Matthew 6:34

How Do We Trust God?

Our Lord Jesus is steadfastly committed to us. He is 100% reliable 100% of the time. He is faithful to fulfill His promises when we put our trust in Him. God does not fail, forget, falter, change, or disappoint. Many among us know these things and still struggle to trust God with everything. How, then, do we bridge the gap between the head and the heart, between what we know and how we feel?

Everyone wants to know a secret formula, but in the end there usually isn't one. We get rid of our suspicion that God won't come through for us by trusting in Him. The more we practice trust, the less distrust we have. Then, as He comes through again and again as we persevere in following Him, the evidence of His faithfulness in our lives will become overwhelming. If you don't believe me, I challenge you to find one person age 65 or older who has lived for Jesus with everything they have and yet regrets trusting God. Someone who has trusted God for all of those years will not say that God failed them or didn't come through in His promises. Such a person is almost impossible to find.

Some bitter people will say that they've trusted God with everything, but upon closer examination it isn't true, and they're simply upset about having to give control over to God, over not being the master of the universe themselves.

God will always show Himself faithful to the Christian who puts his trust in Him, weathers the storm, and waits for God's deliverance, provision, or guidance.

> *Know therefore that the Lord your God, He is God, the faithful God, who keeps His covenant and His lovingkindness to a thousandth generation with those who love Him and keep His commandments.*
> —Deuteronomy 7:9

> *God is faithful, through whom you were called into fellowship with His Son, Jesus Christ our Lord.*
> —1 Corinthians 1:9

Let us hold fast the confession of our hope without wavering, for He who promised is faithful.

—Hebrews 10:23

If we are faithless, He remains faithful, for He cannot deny Himself.

—2 Timothy 2:13

For as many as are the promises of God, in Him they are yes; therefore also through Him is our Amen to the glory of God through us.

—2 Corinthians 1:20

THE APPLICATION

Trusting in God may initially cost something—the loss of a friend, ridicule, or an abandoned business opportunity—but ultimately, you will reap the blessings of God's promises and you will not be disappointed.

Over 35 years ago I went forward at a Sunday night service and made a decision to trust Jesus with my life. It wasn't that I was not already born again; I was. The decision to let God direct my steps and to trust in His Word has set on fire the course of my life. My testimony is only one among millions of others who have trusted God with their lives and have reaped His grace and blessing, finding purpose, vision, and the desires of their hearts (Psalm 37:4). It is now much easier for me to trust God because I have years of experience to look back on and see that every time I've trusted Him it's turned out for the best (and the times I haven't trusted Him didn't end so well).

We have to decide to trust God many times, but it gets easier the more we do it. Collect a lifetime's worth of testimonies of God's faithfulness. Persevere in His ways and discover the blessings that can be gotten no other way. If you want to marry the right person, have a good marriage and obedient children, if you want to make good decisions, be a success and experience fulfillment, if you want God to bless your finances, if you want to look back on your life and see God's hand, do it God's way.

The elephant in the room is that we wonder whether our own rough estimations are better than God's perfect plumb line. God's perfect standard will never lead us astray, because He, unlike us, is infallible.

Start trusting in God and don't lean on your own understanding (Proverbs 3:5), and He will never let you down.

> *For the Scripture says, "Whoever believes in Him will not be disappointed."*
>
> —Romans 10:11

CHAPTER 2

How to Be Free from the Past

This I recall to my mind, therefore I have hope. The Lord's lovingkindnesses indeed never cease, for His compassions never fail. They are new every morning; great is Your faithfulness.

—Lamentations 3:21–23

Jeremiah was a Jewish prophet who wrote two books of the Old Testament, Jeremiah and Lamentations. He was known as "the weeping prophet," and in fact the word "lamentations" means to cry out or to declare one's sorrows. His reputation was well earned.

In the Book of Jeremiah, the prophet's job was to send warning to the nation of Israel that if they did not turn from their wicked ways, if they did not remember God and follow Him, judgment would come upon them. The Israelites had turned to idolatry and sin, no longer trusting in God's perfect standard but rather trusting in their own appetites and desires. Jeremiah pleaded with the nation to turn back to God, but the Israelites were unrepentant. They did not change their ways. They did not cry out to God for forgiveness.

Thus, in December of 589 BC, judgment came, and its name was Babylon. Under King Nebuchadnezzar, the Babylonian Empire attacked Jerusalem, slaughtered its people, destroyed Solomon's temple, and ransacked its riches. Of those that survived, many were carried away into bondage to a far and foreign country. King Zedekiah of Israel was forced to watch his sons' executions just before the Babylonians put out his eyes, so that the last sight he would ever have seen was that horrid tragedy. Then, they carried him off to Babylon. Only a small, frightened, defeated remnant remained in Israel. The rest had either been carried off to another nation or destroyed.

Judgment was far worse than Jeremiah could have imagined.

I have to wonder if Jeremiah might have felt like a failure. He spent years proclaiming warnings and predicting horrible future events if the people did not repent, but they didn't listen to him. Though he did his job and certainly bore no responsibility in the calamity that came upon Jerusalem, the tragedy of witnessing all he had ever known and loved burned and broken must have weighed heavily on his soul. When the dust had settled, Jeremiah and the few others who remained were facing an uncertain future, overshadowed by the horrors of the recent past.

The Book of Lamentations was written just after the Babylonians returned to their country, having destroyed or stolen the best of Israel. Like its name implies, much of it is Jeremiah declaring his sorrows, weeping for his lost countrymen, crying out to God in the confusion and the heartbreak. Israel was ruined, and so was Jeremiah.

However, in chapter three a shift happens. Jeremiah begins to remind himself of God's faithfulness and of His great mercies.

> *"The Lord is my portion," says my soul, "Therefore I have hope in Him." The Lord is good to those who wait for Him, to the person who seeks Him.*
> —Lamentations 3:24–25

Hidden inside of these verses is one of the most magnificent truths of Christianity: If you follow the Lord, then He is working in your life. No matter what else is going on or how terrible things have been, God does not and will not abandon you. Because there is a shift in

Jeremiah's thinking, perhaps he remembered the words that the Lord gave him to write down earlier:

> *"For I know the plans that I have for you," declares the Lord, "plans for welfare and not for calamity to give you a future and a hope."*
>
> —Jeremiah 29:11

Even in judgment God had not abandoned His people. God did not delight as the Israelites faced the consequences of their sins. He tried to warn them what would happen if they continued in their folly. Even after they did not listen, God still had a plan for the future. He brought the Israelites back to their native land, as we read in the books of Nehemiah and Ezra, and restored the righteous law in their civilization. They were blessed as a result.

> *"As I live!" declares the Lord God, "I take no pleasure in the death of the wicked, but rather that the wicked turn from his way and live. Turn back, turn back from your evil ways! Why then will you die, O house of Israel?"*
>
> —Ezekiel 33:11

Sometimes we make the mistake of thinking that God is waiting for us to mess up, or that His mercy for us runs out—even if we are in Christ Jesus. This couldn't be further from the truth. God gave hope to His prophet and to His people. God desired their success and He desires yours too. His mercies are new every morning.

PAUL'S STORY

The apostle Paul had a dreadful past. How could you get any worse? He fought against God's people and opposed the preaching of the gospel. He rounded up Christians and put them in jail. He essentially held their coats as the Jews stoned Stephen. The blood on Paul's hands was thick. He was responsible for the murdering of many innocent Christians who had committed no crime other than following Jesus. As a Pharisee, he ravaged the Church of God.

According to his own words in 1 Timothy 1:15, Paul believed himself to be chief among sinners.

And yet, God used Paul in a powerful way. Not only did Jesus appear to him and cause him to repent, but he gave his entire life to God. Paul wrote most of the New Testament and planted the churches that were responsible for taking the gospel into most of the world. The Lord spoke to him and through him. He was empowered with powerful gifts of the Holy Spirit. He trained up the next generation of church leaders and saints. Even today we feel the impact of the work that God did through Paul.

How is this possible?

Paul could have been crippled by his past. What do you do with that sort of guilt? The guilt of murder and oppression must have come into his mind now and then, and believe me, once he got saved there were plenty of people in the church who didn't want him to forget who he had been and what he had done. I'm sure there was someone who was always reminding him of his sins, someone who couldn't wait to get rid of him. As a matter of fact, when he got to Jerusalem, it wasn't long before the church leaders put him on a boat and said, "See ya. God bless. Bye." No one contacted him for 7 or 8 years, though he was willing to serve. It would have been easy for Paul to capitulate, to give in to despair and the belief that God hated him. Instead, he wrote these words:

> *Brethren, I do not regard myself as having laid hold of it yet; but one thing I do: forgetting what lies behind and reaching forward to what lies ahead, I press on toward*

*the goal for the prize of the upward call of God in Christ
Jesus.*

—Philippians 3:13–14

Everyone has a past. Failure is simply a part of the human
experience. Tragedy happens to us all at some point. The important
thing is to remember that God doesn't define us by our pasts if we look
to Him. Remember what 1 John 1:9 tells us:

*If we confess our sins, He is faithful and righteous
to forgive us our sins and to cleanse us from all
unrighteousness.*

—1 John 1:9

"All unrighteousness" means everything. God wipes away our
transgressions when we come to Him for forgiveness. He doesn't
remember our sins anymore. When we approach Him with repentance,
He casts our sins as far away from Himself as the East is from the West.
It's no wonder, then, that God could use and embrace somebody like
Paul the Pharisee, Paul the murderer. Paul had a radical encounter with
Jesus, and the Lord washed all of his sins away.

The past only defines us if we allow it. Our identity in Christ ought
to be how we look at ourselves, not as the hosts of past transgressions.

BEATING YOURSELF UP

For those of you who do not know me, I am what you might call an
emotional person. I have loads of energy. Sometimes all of this energy
and passion gets ahead of the clear thinking part of my mind and I
stick my foot in my mouth. I can't tell you how many times I've gone
and said something rash or stupid over the years. Walking away from
one particular situation where I had said something rash, I remember

thinking, "David, do you hate yourself? Why on earth would you say something so foolish?"

This sort of thing used to keep me up all night, and not just for one night either. I can't tell you all of the sweat and energy and useful hours I've burned up fretting about some dumb error I had made. As a pastor, when you say something with less than perfect tact, you get letters, and I've gotten those letters. What people don't seem to realize is that nobody beats up David Hoffman like David Hoffman. I've never needed the reminder. By the time someone else complains about something I've done, I'm already in the third act of an internal drama titled "Woe Is Me."

Though this may be my inclination, thank God that I do not live this way anymore. It took me many years to figure out what God has been saying plainly all along, but I'm so glad that I finally got it.

Forgiveness is freedom. Take a moment and say it out loud: Forgiveness is freedom.

Jesus took my failures, your failures, the stupid things we've done, and He put them upon Himself on the cross so that we could live in freedom. It's not just something we sing about; it's real. If you have asked for forgiveness, your sin isn't even on Jesus' mind when He looks at you. All that the God of the universe is thinking about each morning when He looks at you is, "What can we do with today?" What matters to Jesus is how I act today. Yesterday is history.

I've been a pastor long enough to know that I am not the only one who is an expert at beating himself up.

I've sinned against people. I've disobeyed God. I've missed opportunities. I've said foolish things. If you are honest with yourself, you ought to be nodding along with me, because everyone has done those things at one time or another. So we start rehearsing our foolishness in our minds over and over, beating ourselves up, but there is a problem: It doesn't help. It doesn't make us any more holy, it doesn't help us to avoid the same mistakes in the future, and it doesn't help us get anything productive done. Jesus offers forgiveness, and in that forgiveness is freedom from guilt, lies, accusations, feelings of failure and hopelessness, and freedom from what anyone else thinks.

None of what you or I have done can keep us from the precious love of Jesus or the forgiveness of God. No hateful letters, no accusations, no mistakes, and no opinions can cause you to forfeit the anointing and freedom that God has for you. All that can keep us from these things is an unwillingness to get forgiveness or an unwillingness to walk in that forgiveness.

Jesus already died. We don't need to crucify Him again. Every morning the Lord's compassions are new, and He is faithful to do as He said.

EVERY DAY IS A NEW BEGINNING

A lot of people wake up feeling depressed or anxious, and most of them probably think that they're the only ones. I used to be the same way, either worried over some tragedy happening around me like Jeremiah or worried over my sinful past like Paul. The truth found in Lamentations 3:21-23 has set me free from all of that.

Every day when I wake up, I say aloud, "This is the day that the Lord has made. I will rejoice and be glad in it!" (Psalm 118:24). Particularly when there is some issue in my life that I'm having to deal with, I remind myself that God's mercies are new every single morning. "Lord, You made this day. You have anointed this day. You want me to enjoy this day and to have success in it."

God wants us to conquer each day. He wants us to succeed. Even if yesterday was a mess, today is a fresh start because it isn't how you start that matters but how you finish. There are no medals handed out for the runner who came quickest out of the gates. It's only the runner who crosses the finish line who receives the prize, and that ought to encourage those of us with tragedy or errors in our pasts. Today is brand new, and God wants me to live it well.

Today is a gift.

Every day I pray that the Lord would help me not to say, do, infer, or write anything that brings shame to Him, His kingdom, or my family. Some days I accomplish that desire, others I fail. Yet even on nights when I've had a rough day and I go to bed kicking myself, I'm waiting for that first light of dawn. I can't wait to see daylight break, because I know a new day means a new start. Jesus has forgiven me, and all He really cares about is how I love Him today, how I trust Him today, how I obey Him today.

If you can see these truths and commit to living your life this way, it will revolutionize everything. The sooner you get the truth of God's love and forgiveness toward you, the better off you will be. Nothing can separate you from His love if you reach for Him. Even in the midst of tragedy He is working on your behalf.

Every day is a second chance.

This I recall to my mind, therefore I have hope. The Lord's lovingkindnesses indeed never cease, for His compassions never fail. They are new every morning; great is Your faithfulness.

—Lamentations 3:21–23

Paul was content behind bars

CHAPTER 3

How to Be Content

I have learned to be content in whatever circumstances I am. I know how to get along with humble means, and I also know how to live in prosperity; in any and every circumstance I have learned the secret of being filled and going hungry, both of having abundance and suffering need.

—Philippians 4:11–12

It all came to a head as we were driving one day, and I was griping. My wife Mary suddenly looked at me and said, "Dave, when you complain about not being able to buy something or take a vacation, you make me feel like our children and I are a burden to you. Maybe you feel like you'd be better off without us. Can't you just learn to be content and be happy with how God is providing for us?" *Dawg ina*

Immediately I started to get angry. I thought, "I'm a pastor! I've forgotten more about contentment than you'll ever learn. I've preached on it! Someone needs to remind you of that passage about taking the log out of your own eye…" As the day passed, I began to realize that, darn it, she was right. I wasn't happy. I was extremely discontented.

Our church is run by my brother Mark and me, and for years, though we had two pastors, we could not afford to pay two pastors. Then, once we started growing, we had to hire a larger staff, and of course we had to take care of them first, so we couldn't give ourselves a raise. I remember crying out to God, "This is why I didn't want to become a pastor in the first place!" I didn't want to be poor. That day in the car, all those years ago, I truly believed we were poor.

Truth be told, I was just tired of fixing things. Whenever something would break, I'd get a call. Since we couldn't afford to hire somebody, I'd have to quit working, come home and tinker around with the car or the sink or the pipes, and then inevitably I'd make it worse, get angry about having to be the one to fix it in the first place, and this sort of spiraled on. I wanted to be able to have a trailer so I could take my kids camping. I didn't want to have to worry about money all of the time, and I started getting sarcastic with God.

Don't do that. Take my word for it—don't get sarcastic with God.

"God," I said, "I mean really! If this is the way You treat people who are trying to commit themselves to You, I'm surprised that anybody serves You!"

I was in a bad place. When my wife challenged me that day, finally fed up with my attitude, I realized that something needed to change in my thinking or I would be miserable my whole life.

CIRCUMSTANCES

I, Paul, write this greeting in my own hand. Remember my chains. Grace be with you.
—Colossians 4:18 NIV

For which I am an ambassador in chains.
—Ephesians 6:20

The apostle Paul wrote at great length about contentment. He wrote a number of encouragements to the church to live in joy and happiness.

What struck me, when I really began to dig into this for my own life, was that Paul preached about contentedness from behind bars.

I don't think I need to remind you that an ancient Roman jail cell was not like the prisons of today, where at least inmates are guaranteed certain rights and certain kinds of treatment. Throughout the course of Paul's ministry, he had been beaten, whipped, stoned (had rocks thrown at him until they thought he was dead), shipwrecked three times, hungry, tired, thirsty, without a resting place, and imprisoned many times (2 Corinthians 11). Yet despite all of this, Paul was not angry with God. He did not feel that he was being treated unfairly, and he didn't dwell on his pains. He says instead:

> *But I rejoiced in the Lord greatly, that now at last you have revived your concern for me; indeed, you were concerned before, but you lacked opportunity. Not that I speak from want, for I have learned to be content in whatever circumstances I am. I know how to get along with humble means, and I also know how to live in prosperity; in any and every circumstance I have learned the secret of being filled and going hungry, both of having abundance and suffering need.*
>
> —Philippians 4:10–12

What this taught me is that contentment is not only possible in any situation, it can be *learned*. The definition of "contentment," then, is the ability to enjoy life, regardless of circumstances.

ARE YOU DISCONTENTED?

Fill in this blank for me: I will be happy when I will have laynие.

Some common responses are things like, "I will be happy when I get a promotion at work," "When I get a raise," "When I get pregnant,"

"When I have a nice car," "When I get married," etc. Friend, let me share an important truth with you. If your happiness depends on the word "when," you'll never be happy. It's a dead giveaway that somewhere in your heart, discontent is alive and well.

Beyond this simple diagnosis, let's look at the issue further. If most people have a "when" clause attached to their happiness in life, the unasked question is, "What if it never happens?" What if that blank you filled in never comes to pass? Are you going to spend your life being miserable? If you want a wife, God may call you to singleness. Does that mean you won't ever be happy? If you want a Lamborghini, but life circumstances never allow it, what will that do to your joy?

Suppose that your blank does come to pass. Then what? Will you suddenly stop tying your happiness to achievement of some desire? There's always another promotion after that first one, isn't there? There's always another raise to get, a newer car, a fresher look, etc.

U.S. News and World Report did a study in 1999 about the American Dream.[1] They asked thousands of people, "What would you need in your life right now to experience the American Dream?" The number one answer was, "To make twice as much money as I make right now." Think about that for a second. The people they asked did not all have the same income; they were over a wide spectrum. I think we're all smart enough to figure out that anyone who thinks they'll be living the dream once their salary doubles will have the same gripe even if it does. If we were to ask these same people the same question a few years down the road, I'm betting that even if they had doubled their salary, they would still say, "Double my salary." We're never satisfied when we think this way.

---

[1] Archives from U.S. News and World Report that are this old have proven difficult to find and navigate, thus this information comes from my memory of it.

3 Steps to Learning Contentment

One of the most common creeds in American (and many other parts of the world) today is, "I just want to be happy." We say that, but we apparently don't believe it. Happiness is not the highest good (that's a subject for another day), but even in our culture that believes it is, so many people are miserable. Americans spend over $70 billion on the lottery every year.[2] $70 billion! Yet if people really valued happiness above materialism, they would flee from the lottery. Have you ever read about past lottery winners? Almost without exception it ruins their lives. It's astonishing how miserable a sudden windfall like this can make a person, and yet we continue to believe that the money will make us happy.

The Book of Proverbs gives us a different picture.

> *Better is a dry morsel and quietness with it than a house*
> *full of feasting with strife.*
> —Proverbs 17:1

Truly, there are some things that money can't buy. There are some problems that an accomplished career cannot erase. There is pure joy that no human relationship, feat, or possession can attain.

If we can learn to be content, we will avoid the world's problem of constantly chasing after happiness and being disappointed. If we can learn to value what truly delights our souls instead of what the world says will make us happy, then circumstances can't touch our joy.

The question remains, how do we learn to be content? There are three steps.

---

2   Isidore, Chris. "We Spend Billions on Lottery Tickets. Here's Where All That Money Goes." *CNN Money,* Aug. 24, 2017. Money.cnn.com/2017/08/24/news/economy/lottery-spending/index.html

Step 1: Reject Materialism

Then He said to them, "Beware, and be on your guard against every form of greed; for not even when one has an abundance does his life consist of his possessions."

—Luke 12:15

He who loves money will not be satisfied with money, nor he who loves abundance with its income. This too is vanity.

—Ecclesiastes 5:10

As a pastor, I've been on a lot of missions trips and I've seen a lot of people come back from them, too. What I always hear when a team comes back from an impoverished country is, "They're so happy there! They have nothing and yet they're just so joyful all of the time." When people come back saying this, it's like their minds have been blown— and for good reason. Seeing happiness and poverty in the same person is anathema to what we are taught every day by our culture. It runs counter to our materialistic conception that excess creates happiness. The opposite is actually true.

It isn't that wealth or abundance keep us from happiness, it's that trusting in excess to make us happy leaves us unsatisfied. Wanting "more" is an endless cycle.

Now, I want to clarify something. Working to make a better life for your family is not necessarily materialism, nor is seeking to accomplish great things in your career, or even buying a certain thing. Contentment is not apathy. Materialism ties our possessions with our happiness, and contentment severs that tie.

Material things cannot bring us lasting happiness.

The most poignant example I know of that illustrates this principle involves a basketball player by the name of Pete Maravich.

For those of you who aren't basketball fans, Pete Maravich was the greatest college basketball player of all time. He still holds the all-time scoring record in the NCAA, having scored 3,667 points over his time at LSU. Not only does this record from 1970 still stand (a sports record standing for nearly 50 years is almost unheard of), but he set the scoring record before the three point shot had been established, before the shot clock increased scoring in every game, and when freshmen weren't allowed to play varsity sports. He scored 3,667 points in college in only three years, was named player of the year by a number of different sporting organizations, and his jersey was retired by LSU.

Basketball was Pete's life. It was all he ever wanted to do. By the time he was in junior high school, still just a small child, he was so good that he played on the high school's varsity squad—and he was their best player. He wanted to become the first professional basketball player to make $1 million a year.

After his incredible tenure in college, Pete Maravich went into the NBA and eventually became the first player to earn $1 million a year, just as he wanted. This is to say nothing of the five seasons he was named an NBA all-star, the season he led the league in scoring, his 68 point game (only six players in history have scored more in an NBA game), his ten incredible years in the league, and his jersey being retired by three professional teams (including a team he didn't play for—he's one of only four players in history to hold such an honor). Pete accomplished everything. He was a superstar among superstars. He got everything he ever wanted.

And yet he often found himself locked in his bedroom, curtains closed, fighting a losing battle against crippling depression and an overwhelming urge to die.

Pete Maravich had "destination sickness." His dreams did not satisfy.

Thankfully, after a couple of very dark years, Pete came to faith in Jesus and found joy in life again, but the story of his dissatisfaction has a lot to teach us.

If you want to have contentment in your life, you have to reject materialism as a core value. You must recognize and live in accordance with the truth that awards, possessions, and money are not what will make you happy. You need to accept what God says about money and reject the urge to value it above everything else.

People often say, "I just can't live on what I make!" Usually what they mean is, "I just can't live the lifestyle I think I deserve on what I make!" That's what gets so many of us in trouble with credit cards. When I hear people talk this way, I am reminded of the story about the man who went to live in a monastery to pray and get his life back on track. A monk showed him to his room and said, "I hope you have a wonderful stay. If you need anything, don't hesitate to ask, and we'll explain to you how to live without it."

We have to stop saying, "If only…." I am not saying you shouldn't better your financial situation for your family. You should! I am not saying it is more spiritual to be poor. It isn't! Some of the most spiritual people I've met in my life are very wealthy and generous. The point is that we must reject the idea that wealth, prestige, power, possessions, or career can make us happy.

Step 2: Trust God

> *But godliness actually is a means of great gain when accompanied by contentment. For we have brought nothing into this world, so we cannot take anything out of it either. If we have food and covering, with these we shall be content.*
>
> —1 Timothy 6:6–8

We have already discussed the necessity and the blessing of trusting God (chapter 1). Instead of rehashing what we already talked about, I want to point your attention to an often-overlooked definition: Trusting in God means pursuing godliness.

"Godliness" simply means trusting God enough to get up every day and live for Jesus. It's understanding that when we mess up, we ask forgiveness from the Lord and from anyone involved, and the next day we wake up full of grace and forgiveness again. It is living in humility, not thinking more highly of ourselves than we should (Romans 12:3).

Godliness is not complicated. It means that we live for Jesus.

To trust God means that we surrender to Jesus in all things. As we recognize that God is sovereign over everything that we have, we can come to the altar and lay down our wishes, dreams, and everything in our lives at the feet of the Lord. Then we can truly say, "God, it's up to You. I want Your way. I want to live for You, so it's Your purpose, Your timing, Your plan." Then, contentment begins growing in our hearts.

Step 3: Be Thankful

Without thankfulness, I don't think it's possible to live in contentment for long. With a heart of thankfulness, however, it is nearly impossible to remain discontented. When we make a daily practice of thanking God for His love, for His provision, His reliability, His guidance, His peace, our spouses, our children, our jobs, and our lives, it changes everything. It changes our attitudes. It reminds us of what is really important.

We live in sort of a rural area, so getting from my house to the freeway takes a few minutes. Every day when I get in the car, I'm repeating the verse, "This is the day Lord has made. I will rejoice and be glad in it." By the time I get to a street called Manzanita, I'm thanking God for everything I can think of. I always thank God for my wife, even if we've just had a spat. It's funny; once I begin thanking God for all the wonderful things about my wife, I can't be hardhearted toward her any longer. My wife has gotten a lot of phone calls from me over the years by the time I get to the office, telling her that I'm sorry or how much I love her.

If you have a house full of children that are driving you crazy, start thanking God for your kids. Thank Him for the various aspects of your children's lives and personalities, and it will completely shift your perspective. Being thankful has the power to change your attitude from hopelessness, fear, and anxiety, to hope and delight in the future.

The last thing we need to understand about thankfulness before we can really grab a hold of it is that it's a choice. Thankfulness can be chosen in any circumstance.

In the Book of Acts, chapter 28, the apostle Paul is in prison in Rome. I would imagine that he understood very acutely that only three things could happen to him: they could release him, they could sentence him to a lifetime of hard labor in exile, or they could execute him. His friend Luke records a telling scene, amidst the turmoil that must have been on his mind:

> *And the brethren, when they heard about us, came from there as far as the Market of Appius and Three Inns to meet us; and when Paul saw them, he thanked God and took courage.*
>
> —Acts 28:15

Paul's attitude changed completely, and Luke saw it. He thanked God. He took courage. Being thankful is a powerful choice.

PRACTICE

Learning to be content is not easy, but it is absolutely possible, no matter what circumstance you are in. First you have to tell yourself that it is possible to learn to live above your situation. Whenever you start thinking, "If only…" stop and remind yourself that Jesus is the way, the truth, and the life, and that material things will never satisfy your heart. Practice living each day for Jesus. Give thanks continually, ensuring that you have a time to regularly praise God. Even if it's just the ten-minute drive after dropping the kids off at school, thanking God will have a powerful impact on your life.

If you do these things, you won't only learn how to be content on an intellectual level, you will feel it in your heart. Then, like the apostle Paul, you will be able to say:

> *I have learned to be content in whatever circumstances*
> *I am. I know how to get along with humble means, and*
> *I also know how to live in prosperity; in any and every*
> *circumstance I have learned the secret of being filled and*
> *going hungry, both of having abundance and suffering*
> *need.*

> —Philippians 4:11–12

CHAPTER 4

How to Wait

---

*For from days of old they have not heard or perceived by
ear, nor has the eye seen a God besides You, Who acts
in behalf of the one who waits for Him.*

—Isaiah 64:4

Have you ever been to the circus? It may not be as popular today as it once was, but if you've ever seen one, you know it's phenomenal. The magicians, the elephants, the jugglers, and trick riders all astound the audience, but for me, nothing beats the flying trapeze.

If you aren't familiar with the term, a flying trapeze is basically two or more suspended bars that can swing back and forth way above the ground. They're sort of like swings, if Stephen King had invented swings. One false move from that height and you're dead. Pretty scary for a swing. But the acrobats take it a step further. They get up a bunch of speed, and then they *let go*. Sometimes they even twist and flip around as they're soaring through the air. Then, just at the last possible second, another acrobat swings in and catches the flying partner by his outstretched hands.

There weren't even any nets when we used to go see the flying trapeze as kids. The discipline and precision of the performers still astounds me, but beyond the spectacle, I always wonder what must be going through the flying partner's mind before he's caught. Since he's flipping around and often going backwards, he can't see his catching partner. His job is to hold his hands out and wait to be caught. If he tries to catch the catcher, the connection will miss and he will fall to his death. Of course, he can't just keep his arms at his sides either. The flyer has to stretch out as far as he can and trust in his partner to do the rest.

That moment of helpless waiting strikes me as significant for our Christian walk. The flying acrobat can't panic and he can't despair. If he wants his partner's help, he just has to hold out his hands and wait.

If I'm a trapeze artist, my first question is certainly, "Can I trust my catcher?" Well, God is our catcher. In life's moments of suspended gravity, can we trust Him?

THE IN-BETWEEN

Trust in the Lord with all your heart and do not lean on your own understanding. In all your ways acknowledge Him, and He will make your paths straight.

—Proverbs 3:5–6

And we know that God causes all things to work together for good to those who love God, to those who are called according to His purpose.

—Romans 8:28

The Bible is full of wonderful promises that God gives to His people. He tells us that He will instruct us and counsel us (Psalm 32:8), that those who trust in Him will not be disappointed (Romans 10:11), that His plans for us are good and not evil (Jeremiah 29:11). In chapter 1 we discussed this at length. God is trustworthy and His promises are true, but there is an in-between. Between the promise believed and the promise fulfilled is a period of waiting. It wouldn't be a promise otherwise—it'd be a statement. Waiting is an inherent, inseparable part of promises.

That doesn't sit well with most of us Americans. We like things instantly. In the Bible, however, we see that waiting is part of walking with God. Contrary to how we often feel about it, it's actually a blessing because, as Isaiah 64:4 tells us, God acts on our behalf as we wait for Him.

Everybody waits. To wait well, without panicking, without despairing, this is what you need to understand:

When you wait on God, you position yourself to be blessed by Him. If you don't wait, you go ahead of God, so to speak. That means you're relying on your own understanding, which means you'll make mistakes. Mistakes have consequences. Consequences are hard, and even worse, we can miss out on the blessing when we don't wait for God.

I hate waiting.

Knowing this doesn't make waiting easy. We all want God to act swiftly, decisively, and to give us progress reports. Often when we don't see progress (or when things are getting worse) we panic and conclude that we better do something before the situation decays completely. As Christians, however, we have to learn how to wait because God's timing is perfect. Our timing, to put it gently, is not.

> *"For My thoughts are not your thoughts, nor are your ways My ways," declares the Lord. "For as the heavens are higher than the earth, so are My ways higher than your ways and My thoughts than your thoughts."*
>
> —Isaiah 55:8–9

ABRAHAM'S IMPATIENCE

Abraham was a great man. He believed God, and God accounted it to him for righteousness (Galatians 3:6). He was the father of a great nation, the forerunner of the faith, the founder of Israel, and God's honored servant. Yet even he struggled with the in-between of God's promise and the fulfillment.

God had told him that he was to be the father of a mighty nation, that his descendants would be as numerous as the stars in the sky, as the dust of the earth (Genesis 12-15). The only issue in Abraham's mind was that the years kept rolling by. Abraham finally decided that he ought to consider his kinsman Eliezer as his heir, but God told him no. He was going to be the father of a great nation. His descendants would be many.

More years passed, and Abraham was now an old man. He had lived in Canaan for ten years, and they were still childless. Then his wife Sarah had a brilliant idea: She advised him to produce an heir through her maidservant Hagar (Genesis 16). I can only imagine the shocked expression on his face when she suggested this, but instead of waiting on God, he went with Sarah's plan. Hagar gave birth to a son named Ishmael. Then, after more years passed, Abraham and Sarah gave birth to a son named Isaac, just as God promised. The strife between Abraham's two sons was so terrible that he eventually had to send Hagar and Ishmael away, and to this day the Jews (Isaac's descendants) and the Arabs (Ishmael's descendants) continue to fight with one another, which has caused all sorts of death and destruction. This is to say nothing of the devastating effect the existence of Ishmael must have had on Abraham's marriage.

He went ahead of God and made things worse. Thankfully, God in His mercy still held up His end of the deal, but Abraham's impatience created a lot of pain and suffering that could have been avoided.

DAVID'S CONSTANCY

David's period of waiting was no less extreme, but the outcome was quite different. At a young age, most likely when he was anywhere from 8 to 15 years old, Samuel the prophet came to Bethlehem and anointed David King of Israel. Then the years started to add up.

He had to grow up, so maybe it didn't get to him at first. But the years kept piling up, and David still wasn't king. Besides, King Saul had sons, natural heirs. How could David ever receive what God had promised? To make matters worse, Saul grew jealous of David's popularity with the people and he became a hunted man. Forced to flee into the wilderness, David, who had once been favored in the king's court, was reduced to leading a band of outlaws. He fled for his life for years, even leaving the country to find safety.

Then, one day when Saul was pursuing David with his warriors, he got too close, and an opportunity presented itself:

> *[Saul] came to the sheepfolds on the way where there was a cave; and Saul went in to relieve himself. Now David and his men were sitting in the inner recesses of the cave. The men of David said to him, "Behold, this is the day of which the Lord said to you, 'Behold, I am about to give your enemy into your hand, and you shall do to him as it seems good to you.'" … So [David] said to his men, "Far be it from me because of the Lord that I should… stretch out my hand against him, since he is the Lord's anointed." David persuaded his men with these words and did not allow them to rise up against Saul. And Saul arose, left the cave, and went on his way.*
> —1 Samuel 24:3–4, 6–7

David had a clear opportunity to speed things up! His followers made a convincing argument that he ought to help God out. Saul was isolated from his army, unaware, and extremely vulnerable, but David would not circumvent God's timing. He chose to wait, even when his pursuer was at his mercy. Some of David's men must have thought he was a fool for waiting. Later, another opportunity to kill Saul arose, and again, David elected to trust in God rather than give in to his own understanding.

He waited on God. Then, at age 30, after 15 to 22 years of waiting, he became king. He waited longer than he might have, but he ruled Israel for 40 years, until the end of his days (2 Samuel 5:4). Had he gone ahead and done things his own way, he would probably not have ruled so long or successfully. As the later history of Israel (and of many other nations throughout history) shows us, becoming king by killing the last king does not make for a stable rule, and it usually ends with another supplanter.

David's rule was strong, successful, and blessed because he did things God's way and in His timing.

WHAT IT MEANS FOR US

Waiting on God is an important spiritual discipline of a person who is after God's own heart. It does not mean procrastinating or abdicating your responsibilities. Waiting on God means acting in accordance with the trust that we claim to have in Him.

The temptation during the in-between times is to think, "Maybe I missed something. I need to do something. God helps those who help themselves." It's easy to think that you're on your own and then to take matters into your own hands. The problem is that when we wrest control of our situations away from God, we delay, miss, or mess with the blessing. You wouldn't pull the steering wheel when someone else was driving, so don't get "ahead" of God.

DANG7

Our perception is limited, finite. We see only what is in front of us and we have the benefit of a few decades of experience. God is eternal. He stands outside of time. He sees yesterday, today, tomorrow, and forever all at once. We see how it looks in one infinitesimal corner of the world, but God sees the big picture: Every city, individual, mountain, stream, ocean, planet, atom, electron, and quark is in God's consciousness at any given time. He is omniscient. It would make sense, then, that what God is doing doesn't seem clear to us sometimes. We don't have all of the information, and we need to trust that He is working while we wait.

I hate waiting. I wish that I didn't, but oftentimes this is a real struggle of mine. But every time that I am tempted to go ahead of God and start making it happen on my own terms, I remember the story of Saul like a cautionary tale.

FliP

A DAY LATE AND A DOLLAR SHORT

In the Book of 1 Samuel, we read about King Saul, who started out as a great king. He sought the Lord through the prophets, he united the people, and he was successful in protecting Israel from their enemies. He had been so successful in fighting against the warlike peoples that surrounded them that the Philistines gathered all of their strength to come together and wipe out Israel.

> *Then the Philistines gathered together to fight with Israel, thirty thousand chariots and six thousand horsemen, and people as the sand which is on the seashore in multitude. And they came up and encamped in Michmash, to the east of Beth Aven. When the men of Israel saw that they were in danger (for the people were distressed), then the people hid in caves, in thickets, in rocks, in holes, and in pits.*
>
> —1 Samuel 13:5–6 NKJV

The situation was bad. Saul was massively outnumbered. He called Israel to rally to him at Gilgal, but the prophet Samuel had instructed him to wait seven days before taking action.

Day 1 went by. Day 2. The people began getting nervous and started abandoning the camp. Day 3. Day 4. Saul watched as this fractured coalition, which was already hanging by a thread, grew smaller every day. He had a few thousand men at first, but by Day 7, he was down to 600. In his eyes, and in any logical mind, his chances for victory had been getting slimmer every day. You can imagine what his generals must have been saying to him: "We have to attack now! We're losing men every day. Saul, you have to do something!"

On Day 7, the pressure got to him. Saul decided to help God out. Instead of waiting for Samuel, Saul went ahead and made the sacrifices to God himself. After all, it was the seventh day and Samuel hadn't shown up.

Then, as he was finishing the sacrifice, Samuel appeared right on time.

> *And Samuel said, "What have you done?" Saul said, "When I saw that the people were scattered from me and that you did not come within the days appointed, and that the Philistines gathered together at Michmash, then I said, 'The Philistines will now come down on me at Gilgal, and I have not made supplication to the Lord.' Therefore I felt compelled, and offered a burnt offering." And Samuel said to Saul, "You have done foolishly. You have not kept the commandment of the Lord your God, which He commanded you. For now the Lord would have established your kingdom over Israel forever. But now your kingdom shall not continue.*
> —1 Samuel 13:11–14 NKJV

Saul's reaction seems reasonable, and that's what's so frightening. It's so easy to justify our disobedience, but the truth of the matter is that Saul had been instructed, and he jumped the gun. Ultimately, it's an issue of control. "Alright, it's almost past the time God told me, so I guess I'm on my own. I will handle this." That is why Samuel told Saul that he had acted foolishly. God did give the Israelites victory over their enemy, but as promised, Saul was removed and his line did not endure in the kingship.

How can we avoid Saul's error? What does it look like for the Christian who wants to wait on God and let Him do His work in His timing?

Steps to Waiting Well

- Surrender idols

- Obey yes

- Watch and Listen

The temptation is to grab control of the situation even in light of God's promises. The solution is to surrender your whole life to Jesus. Pray to Him, "God, I accept Your will in this situation. I give You control. I'll seek counsel. I'll wait on You, Lord, so that this is done according to Your will and not my anxiety."

The next step, obedience, is necessary for two related reasons. First, Jesus says that if we love Him we need to keep His commandments. In John 16, Jesus says that if we love Him and keep His commandments then He will answer our prayers so that our joy will be full. Consequently, obedience puts us in a place to hear from God. When we obey, we aren't running blindly or on our own intuition.

43

Once you have surrendered to God and obeyed Him, simply listen and He will speak to you. He'll speak to you while you praise Him at a worship service, through the Bible, from a sermon, or from an open door or a divine appointment. Don't worry that you might not see an open door for what it is—it's going to sound like a garage door squeaking and grinding all the way up so that you know.

> *But as for me, I will watch expectantly for the Lord;*
> *I will wait for the God of my salvation. My God will*
> *hear me.*
>
> —Micah 7:7

Don't give up on God who hasn't given up on you. He is going to fulfill His promise, even if you can't see it coming. Learn to wait on Him.

THE COMING OF THE HOLY SPIRIT

As I mentioned before, when I am tempted to go ahead of God and do things my own way, I often recall the story of Saul's impatience as a warning. I also remember what happened in Acts 1.

Here's a little background: Jesus was crucified and lay in the ground three days, then He rose again just like He said. He appeared to numerous people over the course of the next 40 days, and He gave His disciples the Great Commission to reach the world with the gospel. But there's a caveat. Just when Jesus' followers were at their most jubilant, ready to conquer the world and proclaim His name, Jesus tells them to stay in Jerusalem and to wait for the Holy Spirit to come upon them.

Then He ascended to heaven, and they had to wait.

To their credit, they did wait, and what happened next was extraordinary. God gave them the gift of His Holy Spirit, without which they certainly could not have accomplished the great mission they had

44

been given. Through the Holy Spirit they spoke powerfully in the face of death and persecution, received supernatural knowledge as to where they ought to minister, and established the Church that endures today and will never end. They needed to wait for the Holy Spirit to come into their hearts and into their work.

I'm sure that they were glad to have waited on God. We ought to wait on Him too. Progress is being made that you cannot yet see. If you remember anything from this chapter, I hope you remember this: The Lord acts while we wait. Say it out loud until it sinks in. Don't panic, trust God, and wait for His promise to be fulfilled.

> *For from days of old they have not heard or perceived by ear, nor has the eye seen a God besides You, Who acts in behalf of the one who waits for Him.*
>
> —Isaiah 64:4

CHAPTER 5

How to Make Wise Decisions

But if any of you lacks wisdom, let him ask of God, who gives to all generously and without reproach, and it will be given to him. But he must ask in faith without any doubting, for the one who doubts is like the surf of the sea, driven and tossed by the wind. For that man ought not to expect that he will receive anything from the Lord, being a double-minded man, unstable in all his ways.

—James 1:5–8

Elisha was the son of a wealthy family who probably never expected his life to be much different from that of his parents. When we first encounter him in 1 Kings 19, he is plowing the field with a yoke of oxen, one of many that the family owned. All of a sudden, Elijah the prophet comes by and throws his mantle over him, effectively choosing him as his follower. Elisha had a choice to make: Leave his comfortable, secure life to follow this man whom he had probably never met before or refuse the call and look after his comforts. Elisha chose to follow with great joy, and God used his life in marvelous, miraculous ways.

There was another young man in the Bible who was called by a well-known individual. A rich young ruler came to Jesus asking what he needed to do to inherit eternal life (Mark 10). Jesus spoke with him, then called him to sell his possessions, leave his old life behind, and follow him. This young man chose to keep his things and his place in the world, and the Bible says he "went away grieving."

All of us will make important decisions in our lives: Who you choose to marry, deciding to leave a safe career, opting for the traditional route, picking a place to live, or standing up to an abuser. All of us have pivotal moments in our lives when options lay before us and we have to choose. The million dollar question is how can we know which choice is best? The decisions we make, make us, after all.

We need wisdom to consistently and reliably make good choices, but wisdom is easier spoken about than obtained. To really understand what good decision-making looks like, we must answer three important questions.

1. WHAT IS WISDOM?

Wisdom is the ability to apply biblical knowledge to real-world situations. The truths taught to us in the Bible are unchanging, immutable, and universal in their usefulness. Whether he knows it or not, a person's wisdom is equal to how much of his decision-making framework reflects God's Word.

In our pluralistic culture, this is a radical idea and considered close-minded. But let us consider what the world says knowledge is: Education. There is nothing wrong with education. I'm a great believer in seeking out knowledge and bettering ourselves through study, but it is not the answer to the pivotal moments in our lives. Knowledge is a car, but wisdom (the ability to apply God's Word to life) is gasoline; you can have the fanciest car in the world, but without fuel it's going nowhere.

As biblical knowledge (and its application) has been pulled from the public sphere in America and the number of people with advanced degrees goes up, I don't see an increase of wisdom. I see moral anarchy, relational brokenness, a mental health crisis, and substance abuse of epidemic proportions.

> *For the wisdom of this world is foolishness before God.*
> —1 Corinthians 3:19

It is only when the principles of God's Word are adhered to that real wisdom grows. This leads us to our next question.

2.   HOW DO I GAIN WISDOM?

Just because you've become a Christian does not automatically make you wise. If it did, we would never hear about Christians doing foolish things. As the Book of Proverbs continually urges us, we must seek wisdom and hold onto it. There are three essential activities that you have to do if you want to become wise: Praying, searching the Scriptures, and seeking godly advice.

Praying

> *You do not have because you do not ask.*
> —James 4:2

The first activity we can engage in to obtain wisdom is simple; just ask for it. James 1:5 makes it abundantly clear that God will give you wisdom if you ask Him for it in faith. God's Holy Spirit can come upon you and shape your understanding, open your eyes, and guide you if you have the humility to come before Him and ask. It's deeper than you may realize—asking for something is an implicit admission that you *lack it*. Otherwise you wouldn't be asking.

Whenever you need wisdom, first ask for it from God, then bring the details of your situation before Him.

Searching the Scriptures

> *Ask, and it will be given to you; seek, and you will find; knock, and it will be opened to you. For everyone who asks receives, and he who seeks finds, and to him who knocks it will be opened.*
>
> —Matthew 7:7–8

Since wisdom is the ability to apply biblical knowledge to real-world situations, it is impossible to gain wisdom without being a student of God's Word. In a general sense, you will benefit greatly from a daily practice of reading the Bible. Have you read it all the way through? Have you memorized any scriptures that seem of particular relevance to your life? Developing a regular discipline of Bible study will give you a background of biblical knowledge that you can tap when you find yourself in a crisis. It's like the old saying goes, "Those who fail to plan, plan to fail." Make a strategy to ensure that you are consistently diving into God's Word and learning more of what He has to say to us.

When you are in that place where you need to make a decision, however, you may not have a clear answer from scripture locked away in your mind. This is when tools such as a concordance (like an index of the Bible) can be very helpful. You can quickly and easily do a search online for scriptures pertaining to a certain topic, and then you can prayerfully consider how they apply to your situation.

Seeking Godly Advice

> *The way of a fool is right in his own eyes, but a wise man is he who listens to counsel.*
>
> —Proverbs 12:15

Sometimes you have a decision to make and you've asked the Lord for wisdom, but you don't have a clear feeling on which way you ought to go and you can't find any scripture on the topic. What do you do?

You go and find an old person who has been a Christian for a while (gray hair is a good indicator). Not every old person is wise, and not every young person is a fool, but there is a richness of insight and experience in somebody who has been walking with the Lord for a long time. More likely than not they will be able to point you toward scriptures you didn't know about, or, failing at that, they can advise you based on what they have learned in a lifetime of living for Jesus.

It should go without saying that not everyone is qualified to be considered godly counsel. But I urge you, find three or four people whom you trust completely that you can ask for advice when a big decision is looming over you. I may be a pastor and I may be the one in front of the church teaching, but I dare not make a major decision without running it past the handful of godly, wise men that I trust the most. These are people who won't just agree with whatever I say; they aren't afraid to tell me when they think I've got it wrong. That's a valuable trait in an advisor, and if you want to be wise, you need to find someone like that who knows God's Word inside and out.

PUTTING IT TOGETHER

It is vital that these three steps are done all together, because we humans are by nature pretty manipulative. It's amazing how often our tests come out with the answer we were hoping for, isn't it? Yet by asking for wisdom and searching the Scriptures and seeking godly counsel, we ensure that self-deception does not creep into our decisions. God's Spirit will never contradict His Word, and mature believers can be a good check on ourselves.

Prayer (asking God for wisdom), searching the Scriptures, and seeking godly advice is a surefire path to wise decision-making, even if the unthinkable happens—you go through all of it and don't arrive at a clear answer. In that instance, after honest, diligent seeking, your job is to get on your knees, tell the Lord what you've done to prepare to make this decision, and then choose something right there, trusting that God has given you the wisdom you asked for.

But God Told Me To!

Beloved, do not believe every spirit, but test the spirits to see whether they are from God, because many false prophets have gone out into the world.

—1 John 4:1

I can't tell you how many times as a pastor I've had someone in my office looking at me with a straight face and telling me that God told them to do some ridiculous thing. "I prayed about it" is not a trump card for ensuring your choice is the right one. I know of a man who "prayed about it" and decided that God told him to leave his wife of over a decade, abandon his children, including one with special needs, and to run away with his (much younger) secretary.

God did not tell that man to do what he did.

The scripture is obvious, written in black and white: *Anyone who divorces his wife and marries another woman commits adultery* (Luke 16:18). This means that wanting a change is not an acceptable reason for divorce and remarriage. Even though this man says that he heard from God, he didn't.

When people tell me, "God told me…" and it becomes clear that He most certainly did *not* tell them, I push back. I'll say, "God is not speaking to you about this," and then I show them scriptures about their situations that help me to know. Occasionally when this happens, they lean up from reading the Bible and say, "Wow. I guess the Lord isn't speaking to me." That is a wise person right there. Usually, however, they only get angry and dig in their heels. Why? Why are they so convinced that their impression in prayer trumps Scripture? Because their supposed revelation is telling them exactly what they wanted to do anyway.

This is why we need to test the spirits, as 1 John tells us. Below is a summary of a section from my book *Prayer Will Change Your World.* It is an eight-fold test for determining whether God is actually speaking to you or not. When you receive a word in prayer, run through this list:

DOES IT AGREE WITH SCRIPTURE?

Ask this question first. God will never, ever contradict Himself because He never changes (Malachi 3:6). He is reliable in the Bible, which will never lead you astray. If you ever find yourself thinking that God has given you a revelation that supersedes His Word, make no mistake, you are in deception.

DOES IT CHALLENGE YOUR FAITH?

Does what you heard in prayer cause you to step out, trust God, and mature in your walk with the Lord? God is always concerned with our sanctification and maturation. If you are challenged to take a step of faith or steps toward holiness, there is a good chance God is speaking to you. The Bible says, *Without faith it is impossible to please Him* (Hebrews 11:6).

DOES IT GO AGAINST WORLDLY WISDOM?

God tells us in Isaiah 55:8–9 that His thoughts are not our thoughts and His ways are not our ways. If you believe that you have received a word from the Lord and it seems illogical, going against worldly wisdom, it could quite possibly be from God. Often what He tells us to do goes against the good advice of the culture. It is as if He is testing us in an effort to increase our faith and trust in His promises.

A word of caution: I am not suggesting that you throw all common sense out the window. This is only one of the signs of hearing God's voice. If you base your discernment of God's voice solely on this one test you will get into trouble fast. However, God will often tell us to do something that goes against worldly wisdom.

WHAT DO MATURE CHRISTIANS SAY ABOUT IT?

Take what you think you've heard from the Lord to other mature Christians for confirmation. A pastor, Bible study leader, elder, or counselor can help you sort out what is scriptural and what isn't, speaking the truth in love and honestly sharing what they think. If God really is speaking to you, mature Christians should be able to recognize God's voice and confirm it.

DOES IT CAUSE YOU TO TAKE A STAND FOR CHRIST?

Does what you think you heard cause a banner to be raised over your life that reads "Follower of Jesus"? Will your coworkers or other nonbelievers see your obedience to Christ? The last thing Satan wants is for us to let other people know we are Christians, proclaiming that Jesus is the only way, truth, and life. Standing up and being counted for Christ brings God's light into the world. If following through with what you think you heard causes you to take a stand for Christ amidst this "evil and perverse generation," it could very well be from God.

DOES IT WANT YOU TO RUSH?

Nowhere in God's Word are we told to rush into anything. Proverbs 19:2 says, *He who makes haste with his feet errs* (NASB 1977). If you believe that you have heard from God to forgo all restraint and rush into something, most likely it is not from God. Satan wants us to act impulsively; God tells us to test the Spirits, to seek wise counsel, and to count the cost.

The devil wants you to go it alone, filled with pride, convinced that you have an exclusive pipeline to God. Then, when things go south, the devil wants you to blame God for your own rash decision. As a pastor, I have seen many Christians make grave mistakes simply because they did not take the time to test what they thought God was telling them. God rarely wants us to rush.

DOES PEACE COME WITH IT?

Initially when we hear God speak to us, we may wrestle with Him, feeling anxiety, fear, or conflict because of what we believe the Lord wants us to do. But, as we pray, seek counsel, and read His Word, this conflict will be replaced with the peace of God if it was actually from Him. That doesn't mean you will be 100% devoid of apprehension, but God will give you peace if you are hearing from Him.

> *Be anxious for nothing, but in everything by prayer and supplication with thanksgiving let your requests be made known to God. And the peace of God, which surpasses all comprehension, will guard your hearts and minds in Christ Jesus.*
>
> —Philippians 4:6–7

DOES IT YIELD GOOD FRUIT?

If what you think you heard brings fear, bondage, anxiety, confusion, lust, or division, then the fruit is evil and the word is not from the Lord. If, on the other hand, you see that the word causes you to grow in faith, develop godly characteristics, and pursue holiness, then it probably is from the Lord.

Examine everything carefully. Then, make a wise decision.

3.   After the Decision, How Can Doubt Disturb Your Peace?

James 1 tells us to ask wisdom from God, but it also gives us a warning not to doubt because doubting will turn us into double-minded people. If you don't know what it means to be double-minded, let my experience help you. I spent much of my life as an expert.

Years ago we needed to repaint the house. I went down to the paint store and got those big fans of paint chips. My wife and I sat down for an agonizing length of time, analyzing every color until we finally came up with one color for the trim and one color for the rest of the exterior. The decision was brutal, but it was made.

But then again… maybe there was a better option. It tortured me. Painting your house is a big commitment. You'll probably have those same colors for a decade or more. I thought I'd better look it over again. The next day my wife found me at the table with the paint chips, agonizing again until I picked better colors. It was over.

Then I couldn't rest. Maybe it wasn't right.

Finally, my wife found me at the table agonizing again and she told me, "I don't care if you paint the house purple, just pick something and stick to it!"

I was double-minded. I made a decision but did not let it rest. I set my mind on something, then continually went back and doubted. A double-minded person is like a man with a compass in his hand and a magnet in his pocket; he'll never find north.

If we ask God for wisdom and then doubt whether we have received wisdom, we are subject to the same fate. Trusting that God will make good on His promise of giving us wisdom is crucial, because if we doubt we will be in such a malleable state of mind that no amount of wisdom would do us any good anyway, not to mention the anxiety and unease that this sort of doubting creates.

> *Brethren, I do not regard myself as having laid hold of it yet; but one thing I do: forgetting what lies behind and reaching forward to what lies ahead, I press on toward the goal for the prize of the upward call of God in Christ Jesus.*
>
> —Philippians 3:13–14

Once we have asked God for wisdom, searched the Scriptures, and sought out godly counsel, our last step is to make a choice and move forward. Paul did not look back, and neither should we. Jesus says in Luke 9:62, "No one, after putting his hand to the plow and looking back, is fit for the kingdom of God." He uses the metaphor of plowing a field because furrows need to be straight. The way you plow a straight furrow is by fixing your eyes on one point ahead. If you look backwards, the oxen will start to veer to the right and to the left, resulting in a crooked, useless row.

Double-mindedness keeps us from being a testimony to the peace and love of Christ, and it hinders us from being a clear picture of God-given purpose in life.

Want to make wise decisions? Go through the three steps we discussed (prayer/asking God for wisdom, searching the Scriptures, seeking counsel), make a choice, and then have the faith to move forward.

> *But if any of you lacks wisdom, let him ask of God, who gives to all generously and without reproach, and it will be given to him. But he must ask in faith without any doubting, for the one who doubts is like the surf of the sea, driven and tossed by the wind. For that man ought not to expect that he will receive anything from the Lord, being a double-minded man, unstable in all his ways.*
>
> —James 1:5–8

CHAPTER 6

How to Pray

You do not have because you do not ask.

—James 4:2

A father watched as his little boy was playing outside in a sandbox with his trucks and his cars. He was making roads, digging tunnels, and building little overpasses out of sticks. Then, in the process of making a new road, the little boy ran into a big rock. He crashed his truck into it, then decided that it had to go. He reached underneath but found that it was too heavy for him to lift. He then sat down on his bottom and put his feet on the rock, trying to push it that way. With this new leverage he managed to get it to the edge of the sandbox, where it thudded to a stop. He kept pushing, but it wouldn't budge, so he stood up, walked over, and stuck his hands underneath. With a big strain he lifted the rock on one side about an inch, then he had to lower it. Gathering his strength, he tried again, and once more the rock lifted about an inch off of the sand, but this time it fell onto his fingers and he screamed out crying.

Almost instantly, there was a shadow over him. It was his father, who quickly grabbed the stone with one hand and tossed it out of the sandbox. "Why didn't you use all of the strength that you had?" the father asked his son. "But I did, Dad!" the little boy replied. "No, Son," the father answered him. "You didn't because you didn't ask me for help."

GOD'S STRENGTH

I love the story about the little boy and the sandbox because it rings so true in each of our lives. No matter how industrious or eager for a challenge we might be, every one of us has reached a point where we've thrown up our hands and said, "It's impossible!" Nevertheless, as the angel Gabriel told Mary in Luke 1:37, nothing is impossible with God.

In James 4:2 we read, "You do not have because you do not ask." These nine words explain the general powerlessness of the average Christian today. If you and I are not praying, then we are not accessing the power of God in our individual circumstances.

I'm here to tell you that we, as Christians, have the privilege of releasing God's power, influence, provision, and guidance into life's difficult situations. When we pray and intercede it pleases God, as Paul reminds us in Hebrews 11:6.

> *Without faith it is impossible to please Him, for he who comes to God must believe that He is and that He is a rewarder of those who seek Him.*

Accomplishing God's will requires God's strength. How do we acquire this strength? Through prayer.

According to polling, at least 79% of Americans believe in prayer of some sort.[3] It's a concept that may even be inherent in mankind, the desire to connect with the supernatural. Unfortunately, however, there is a lot of misunderstanding about what prayer is, how it works, and what to do about "unanswered" prayer. Fortunately, we have not been left without an example.

---

[3] Kinnaman and Stone, "Silent and Solo: How Americans Pray" *Barna,* Aug. 15, 2017. "79% have prayed at least once in the past three months."

JESUS TEACHING ON PRAYER

In the Gospel of Mark, there is a fascinating story that will teach us most of what we need to know about prayer if we look carefully. It comes from chapter 11, shortly after Jesus drives the moneychangers out of the temple and resumes traveling with His disciples.

> *On the next day, when they had left Bethany, [Jesus] became hungry. Seeing at a distance a fig tree in leaf, He went to see if perhaps He would find anything on it; and when He came to it, He found nothing but leaves, for it was not the season for figs. He said to it, "May no one ever eat fruit from you again!" And His disciples were listening... As they were passing by in the morning, they saw the fig tree withered from the roots up. Being reminded, Peter said to Him "Rabbi, look, the fig tree which You cursed has withered." And Jesus answered saying to them, "Have faith in God. Truly I say to you, whoever says to this mountain, 'Be taken up and cast into the sea,' and does not doubt in his heart, but believes that what he says is going to happen, it will be granted him. Therefore I say to you, all things for which you pray and ask, believe that you have received them, and they will be granted you."*
>
> —Mark 11:12–14, 20–24

My favorite part of this incredible passage is, "His disciples were listening." You start talking to a fruit tree, people start paying attention. Here's the amazing thing, the tree did as it was commanded by Jesus. The passage tells us that it was not the season for figs, and I'm betting that Jesus knew that. He did what He did to teach His disciples and us about prayer. There are three main lessons we can pull out of this passage.

1. *Pray About Everything*

> *If you abide in Me, and My words abide in you, ask whatever you wish, and it will be done for you.*
>
> —John 15:7

What areas of your life have you not committed to prayer? Why not? Is it because you're discouraged or you think, "God doesn't care about that"? Sometimes it may even seem pointless to pray, since God already knows everything anyway, but this line of thinking is contrary to Scripture. God has revealed to us that we can have miracle-working power in our lives through prayer. The Bible tells us again and again that there is power in prayer.

> *Again I say to you, that if two of you agree on earth about anything that they may ask, it shall be done for them by My Father who is in heaven.*
>
> —Matthew 18:19

> *Whatever you ask in My name, that I will do, so that the Father may be glorified in the Son. If you ask Me anything in My name, I will do it.*
>
> —John 14:13–14

> *You did not choose Me but I chose you, and appointed you that you would go and bear fruit, and that your fruit would remain, so that whatever you ask of the Father in My name He may give to you.*
>
> —John 15:16

It becomes obvious to me the longer I study the life of Jesus that God wants us to pray about everything. Not only does Philippians 4:6 actually, literally instruct us to "pray about everything," but we see throughout Jesus' life and ministry that He brought all of His concerns to God. Ephesians 5:1 and 1 Corinthians 11:1 instruct us to be imitators of Jesus.

He prayed about everything (even something so seemingly small as His next meal from a fig tree) so we ought to pray about everything as well. J. Oswald Sanders summed up Jesus' prayer life this way:

> Jesus prayed in the morning at the gateway of the day, in the evening when the workday was over. Great crisis was preceded by prayer. Great achievements were followed by prayer. Great pressure of work was a call to extra prayer. Great sorrows were met by prayer. He died praying.[4]

God is our Heavenly Father. He wants to be involved in our lives, just like a good parent is interested in his children, wanting to them to be successful. His perspective is different and higher than ours. We see obstacles, but God sees opportunities, and He is definitely interested.

2 Chronicles 16:9 tells us that God is searching throughout the whole world to strengthen the hearts of those that are completely His, to show Himself strong on their behalf. Nothing is too difficult for God. No trouble you've gotten yourself into, no unforeseen circumstances, no financial burden, relational strain, health challenge, or vision is too difficult for Him. Use all of the strength that you have available to you and pray. Pray about everything.

God has given us prayer because He wants to be involved in every aspect of our lives.

2. *Trust in God's Faithfulness*

The Lord is faithful.

—2 Thessalonians 3:3

---

[4] Sanders, J. Oswald. *The Incomparable Christ.* Chicago, Moody Publishers, 1952. Pgs. 135–136.

Jesus tells us in the passage from Mark that when we pray we need to have faith that God hears us and is going to answer us. James 1:5-8, which we discussed in chapter 5, tells us that we need to have faith without doubting when we ask wisdom of God. Hebrews 4:16 tells us that we can have confident access to God, and Ephesians 3:12 says the same. In Psalm 65:2 (NIV), David addresses God as "You who answer prayer."

Trusting God is evidently an important part of prayer.

We have already seen how the Bible reminds us over and over that God answers prayer. If you are a new Christian and do not know many stories of God's miracle power operating in today's world, ask around and be encouraged by the testimonies of God's people receiving help and wisdom in their times of need. Since we know that God is able and willing to answer our prayers, we must pray with confidence, because double-mindedness is an obstacle to effective prayer. We have to trust in God, who gives us such lavish promises and makes good on them.

You may think that you don't, but you have enough faith to pray, to release God's power, and to move mountains in your life. I'll prove it to you, using an example from Jesus' ministry.

In Luke 5, Jesus had just finished preaching to the multitude from Peter's boat (He had to preach from a boat because of how many people there were crowded on the shore). He asked Peter to row to a deeper part of the lake and throw down the net. Peter didn't want to. The Bible says that he had been fishing all night and all morning, and they hadn't gotten anything. Keep in mind that Peter was a professional fisherman; he knew when fish came around for feeding and when they didn't. He was already cleaning and mending his nets when Jesus came along and made His unusual request. If you know anything about fishing, you know that going to the middle of the lake in the middle of the day is a sure recipe for failure. Nevertheless, Peter said, "Because You say so, we'll go out." I don't think he really thought they would catch anything, but out they went to the middle of the lake, and in went the nets, and sure enough, they caught so many fish that the nets began to break.

What does this teach us about prayer? It was not Peter's unyielding, superhuman power to believe in impossible things that allowed the miracle to take place; he just did what Jesus said. If you and I will trust God enough to simply do what He says (obey and pray), then that is enough faith to release God's power and move mountains that loom over you.

On another occasion, Jesus' disciples came to Him after being unable to cast out a demon (so Jesus cast it out), and asked Him why they had been unable to do the work themselves. Jesus answered them:

> *Because of the littleness of your faith; for truly I say to you, if you have faith the size of a mustard seed, you will say to this mountain, "Move from here to there," and it will move; and nothing will be impossible to you.*
> —Matthew 17:20

A lot of people don't like this verse because it causes problems for their theology. It doesn't cause me any problems, and it shouldn't cause you any, either. Jesus said it this way, and no matter what translation you read it in, the message is clear: With even a tiny amount of faith the most impossible tasks become possible. Jesus is telling us that if you have enough faith to get on your knees and sincerely pray about any situation, He will hear you from heaven and send His power into your life. If need be, He will move a mountain.

Why should we doubt? This is the God Who closed lions' mouths, Who parted the Red Sea, Who caused a virgin to give birth, Who caused the Christian Church to conquer the oppressive Roman Empire without any armies. Is your credit card debt too difficult for Him? Your need for a job? Your desire for a wife or husband?

We can trust Him. We must.

3. *Our Prayers Become Reality*

> *This is the confidence which we have before Him, that,*
> *if we ask anything according to His will, He hears us.*
> *And if we know that He hears us in whatever we ask, we*
> *know that we have the requests which we have asked*
> *from Him.*
>
> —1 John 5:14–15

The apostle John understood that prayer was not some kind of magic spell, a desperate hope, wild experiment, or reckless gamble. John knew from experience that God answers prayer. This is where one of the most painful misconceptions about prayer can be rectified—you may notice that a certain phrase keeps appearing in these scriptures on prayer: "According to His will." The phrasing varies slightly, but go back and look at the scriptures we've talked about and you'll see a pattern. We are guaranteed to receive what we ask for if we ask in accordance with God's will.

A lot of people hear the instruction about faith and stop, not only failing to receive the rest of the Bible's instruction but misunderstanding the part that they do have. Praying in faith does *not* mean gritting your teeth and hoping harder. You cannot rustle up enough feeling to cast the mountains into the sea, you cannot focus intently enough to magically change your financial situation. If you disagree, then you are not following Christianity but mysticism and paganism! These ideas of "focusing" and "manifesting" identify you as the source of power instead of God. Faith is more than a vague synonym for belief. Faith means trusting in God's Spirit and being led by Him. When we pray in faith, we are putting all of our hope in His agency, not in our own ability to hope, focus, or shift reality. It is by confidence in God's ability that we know we will receive whatever we ask according to His will, and that will shift reality. God will do it.

So how do we know if we are praying according to God's will?

First of all, we have Scripture. If your prayer agrees with what the Bible teaches, then you are praying according to God's will. Secondly, when you persevere in prayer, when you continue to pray for the same circumstance time after time, many times your prayer will continue to change. If your faith is truly in God, I believe that His Holy Spirit guides your heart and changes it to align with His. That is powerful! Prayer has the power to line up our will with God's. Then, when you have persevered, you will be praying in agreement with God's will.

I've seen this happen in my own life. To give just one example, when we were praying for a church building many years ago, my prayer changed drastically. When we first started, I prayed, "God, we believe You've called us to the ministry, so please provide a building anywhere from West La Mesa to the ocean. That's our spot." Those of you familiar with the geography of San Diego will know that I was missing out on the entire East County (El Cajon, Spring Valley, Lemon Grove, etc.). I didn't believe we were called there. Maybe I didn't want to think we were called there, but after two years, I found myself praying that God would provide us a church building in El Cajon. As we persevered in prayer, God made His will known and we were able to pray in agreement with it.

HOW GOD ANSWERS PRAYER

Whenever you talk about prayer, there is a great deal of concern about requests that go unanswered. The truth of the matter is that there is no such thing. God always answers our prayers, but He answers prayer in four distinct ways. We can get so focused on one particular way that God might possibly answer us that we miss the answer He is actually giving us. It is vitally important for the Christian to understand God's four answers to prayer:

1. *A Quick Yes*

This is my favorite answer. It's fast, quick, and easy. We ask for something, and God grants our request faster than you can order a Big Mac from McDonald's.

Years ago, my wife and I asked the Lord to provide enough money for us to be able to take a vacation. Just days later one of our church members gave us a financial gift that enabled us to take a much-needed, restful trip. Our prayer was granted quickly, and it was wonderful!

It's exciting to see someone healed in the moment that you pray for them or watch as provision comes instantly, but this is not the only way that God answers prayer. Many people, unfortunately, naively believe this to be the only way God responds to our requests. Such a foolish outlook quickly results in either delusion or disappointment because, more often than not, I have found that God generally answers with one of the other three responses.

2. *Yes, but You're Part of the Solution*

Have you ever been driving on a Saturday afternoon when you passed by a homeless person on the street, so you pray, "God, please send someone to help that person"? It ought to be obvious that you could be the answer to that prayer by parking the car and wandering over, but often in the moment we miss that.

Over the years, husbands and wives have sat in my office and said, "I have prayed for my spouse for years, and nothing's happening. I'm angry at God because He must not be responding to my prayer." Often as I speak further with these individuals, I find that they are filled with anger, selfishness, and bitterness. I believe that what God is telling them when they pray about their marriage is, "Yes, your marriage will change, but it has to start with you." Sometimes people don't want to hear that, so they think, "Oh, no, Lord. You don't understand. My spouse is the problem." Unfortunately, no progress is made in these marriages until they realize that God has shown them a path to having their requests granted. People sometimes miss out on what they ask for because they don't like the answer and ignore it.

You may pray for someone to come to faith in Christ, and God might answer that you need to share the gospel with them. You may pray for healing in your relationship with your mother and God might tell you that you need to forgive her in order for that to happen. As we pray, God shows us, "You're part of the answer here."

When we fail to do what God is asking, our problems never change. If, however, we are honestly seeking God in our prayers, how encouraging to see that He can reveal a path to us!

3. Yes, in a Little While

Sometimes the request is right but the time isn't. In those times, God's answer to our prayer is, "Yes, in a little while." Waiting isn't the easiest thing for most of us, but we see from the Bible that God is faithful to bring His promises to pass.

Sometimes the "little while" is longer than we'd like. Abraham was 100 and Sarah was 90 when God gave them a child! David prayed for years that God would deliver him from his enemies before it finally happened. I don't pretend to understand all of God's reasons for delaying a request that He's going to grant, but I do know that He often takes the opportunity to develop character in us. As we wait, He teaches us patience, endurance, trust, contentment, and submission.

There are occasions when God desires to answer our prayer but will wait until we or others are able to handle the request being answered. As I look back on my life, I'm very relieved that He delayed the answer to some of the prayers I prayed in my twenties until I was more mature.

Remember that God's timing is always best—it's even the best for you. It is easy to complain when God tells us, "Yes, in a little while," but God is not impressed by our own assessments of our lives. He sees from a perfect vantage point and knows the right time to bring the answer, even if it seems to us like we can't wait another day. As an earthly father, I was not intimidated by my toddler son's crying when he wanted to keep hold of the scissors he had found. He couldn't handle them yet.

4. Yes, I Have Heard You, but I Have Something Better in Mind

I've heard that this answer sounds a lot like "no," but before dismissing it, consider the story of Lazarus in John 11.

Mary and Martha came to Jesus distraught because He delayed in coming to them. Both sisters essentially told Jesus, "If You had been here, my brother wouldn't have died" (John 11:21,32). Their earlier pleading seemed unheeded—until Jesus raised Lazarus from the dead. If Jesus had heeded their request right away, Mary, Martha, and the whole town would have missed out on one of Jesus' greatest miracles.

Before the miracle, Mary and Martha would certainly have been tempted to think that Jesus was ignoring them or that He had disregarded their request, but how great was their joy when all was revealed? In 2 Corinthians 12, we are told that Paul did not receive relief from the "thorn" in his side, but God instead gave him a greater gift of sufficiency and understanding.

There are times when the Lord answers our prayer by not giving us what we want so that He can give us something even better. This is not a "no" answer from God.

Years ago I was sitting in my office at the church when a man we'll call John came in, distraught. His wife had just told him that she wanted a divorce, that she had already seen a lawyer, and that she was hoping for an amicable separation.

John was blindsided. He didn't understand how his wife could turn her back on the commitment they had made before God. He was devastated both for himself and for the future of his two children, who were now at risk of growing up in a broken home. John went to his wife again and again, seeking to understand why she wanted the divorce, but each time he came away confused. John was willing to do whatever it took to rebuild their marriage, but his wife was not. She refused to see a counselor or talk it over with friends or pastors.

Instead of giving up, John committed to praying intensely for his wife's heart to be softened. I and many members of the church joined him in praying, but after several months the divorce was finalized. Nevertheless, John was not daunted. He said, "Surely God will soften my ex-wife's heart!"

Then he got a painful phone call. His ex-wife was engaged to be married to someone else in two months' time. This time, John's faith was shaken. He asked me the inevitable question, "Why didn't God answer my prayer? Isn't this according to His will?"

John's experience is not unique in the Christian experience. Many people have diligently sought a good thing in prayer and been disappointed when it didn't happen the way they thought it should. Many people grow bitter at God and walk away from the faith, inviting sin and destruction into their lives since they figure that God doesn't care about them anyway. This is a tragedy, because God's answer was not a "no."

In John's case, he persevered, and since he prayed about everything and trusted in God, he got to see things change over time. Though his marriage was not restored, all areas of his life were abundantly blessed.

He would tell you, "God didn't give me what I wanted, but He gave me much more as He changed my life."

God always answers prayers. If we don't have something, it's because we didn't ask.

Ask your Father to move the rock out of the sandbox. He may say "Yes" and quickly do it, He may say "Yes" and tell you to assist Him, He may tell you that He'll move it in a minute, and He may take you out to a monster truck rally instead of helping you with your sandbox roadway. God is good all of the time, and as we remember what Jesus taught us—to pray about all things, to trust in God, and that our prayers become reality—we can have peace that God is putting His power into our situations.

You don't have because you haven't asked. So ask, and allow God to change your heart as you do.

You do not have because you do not ask.

—James 4:2

CHAPTER 7

How to Find Strength in Weakness

Therefore I am well content with weaknesses, with insults, with distresses, with persecutions, with difficulties, for Christ's sake; for when I am weak, then I am strong.
—2 Corinthians 12:10

As a Christian, you will often hear the term "thorn in the flesh." Some people use it to refer to a hard situation or an affliction in their lives. Others, like my father, use it in regards to people: "That man is a thorn in my flesh." The saying comes from the apostle Paul, who writes about it in 2 Corinthians 12:7–10. We don't know specifically to what Paul was referring when he spoke of his "thorn in the flesh," but we do know that it was a hindrance to him. He prayed to God three times to take it away, and God's response was:

My grace is sufficient for you, for power is perfected in weakness.
—2 Corinthians 12:9

This is a radical concept. How can power be perfected in weakness? How can we be strong when we are weak? Aren't these things opposed to one another? In our culture, the idea of strength coming through weakness is repugnant. We love power. We idolize the strongest and the best. We value individuality, emotional toughness, the self-made man or woman. We have self-help programs on every shelf, and I think we would all agree that most of them don't talk about the need to die to yourself or finding strength in weakness. Our society's advice to someone who is struggling is that the strength is really inside of you. "You're full of potential. The answer to your limitation is right inside you. The real problem is unleashing the potential. You are the answer." Ultimately, our culture's obsession with self, self-esteem, and positive affirmations is really pride.

PRIDE

This aversion to admitting weakness makes it very difficult for many to embrace Jesus as their Lord and Savior. Religion, in so many people's minds, is a crutch that weak people need in order to deal with life, to answer unanswerable questions. "I don't need a crutch," they say. "I don't need religion. I can handle things on my own." The pride of wanting to be self-sufficient in every way keeps a lot of people from coming to God.

> *Pride goes before destruction, and a haughty spirit before stumbling.*
>
> —Proverbs 16:18

If you are a Christian, you've had to humble yourself, get on your knees in prayer, and admit your sins to God. Now you are saved, so the first part of Proverbs 16:18 is dealt with. The second part of this verse, however, should cause every Christian to pause and think for a little bit. You and I can still fall into pride as Christians. It takes many forms, but often it can look like this: You get down on your knees to pray about something, but you've already decided what you're going to do. That isn't letting God into the situation or leaning on His strength. We basically say, "This is what I've decided, God. Bless me."

The unfortunate consequence of pride is that we are limited to our own resources.

Jesus taught us to die to ourselves, Proverbs teaches us to lean not on our own understanding, the Psalms show us how to cry out to God in need, but if we think we can handle it on our own, we're going to stumble and suffer. It is only in admitting our weakness that we can begin to access God's unlimited power and supply. For 15 years, I didn't understand this, and the results were evident.

THE "GREAT ANOINTED ONE"

I got saved when I was 22 years old. My father was a pastor, and having grown up around him and seeing what he had to deal with, I did not ever want to be a pastor. The problem was, the Holy Spirit was tenacious in leading me to become one. I knew in my heart that it was what God wanted for me, but I tried to make a deal with Him instead. "God, listen, I have a solution to our problem. I will be the best church member there has ever been. Whatever church I'm in, the pastor will say, 'Man, I love having Dave in this church.' I promise I'll work for You—I'll lead small groups, help with youth groups, anything You want. Just don't make me a pastor."

So in keeping with my "deal" with God, at 23 ½ years of age I had started a concert ministry at a Lutheran church. It was wildly successful. We'd bring in the best talent that the Christian music scene had to offer, and within six months hundreds of people were attending each week. Kids would come from all over San Diego County to hear the concerts, and I would preach the gospel to them. I thought I was pretty hot stuff, only 24 and already speaking in front of huge crowds. Nobody ever left while I preached, and I knew I was pretty good. I was impressed with myself. As I later found out, however, the most common remarks after I spoke were, "Who let this guy speak?" and then someone would say, "He's the pastor's son." And then heads would nod knowingly. Besides, the reason no one left during my sermons was that I would preach them for 15 minutes halfway through the show. People had to stay if they wanted to hear the rest of the music.

Nevertheless, that was my first ministry, and it was a huge success. I wasn't surprised. I was the great anointed one (never mind that it was the artists that drew the crowds and my preaching was terrible).

REVIVAL ON CAMPUS

I got hired as a teacher and a coach up in Central California, so I moved up there and, remembering my deal with God, I started a Christian club after the first couple of months of school. It was a phenomenal success. Every time we wanted to do an event, we had to use the gym because so many kids would come. Teachers would come around and just ask me about God, kids were getting saved, and by the end of the year 20-25% of the school were members of this club. In my mind, I thought, "Of course it's going this way. I am the great anointed one. I'm doing such great work for the Lord."

It truly was incredible to be a part of all this, but the whole time God continued pounding on my heart to go and become a pastor. I finally relented, and I thought, "Alright, God. I don't want to, but fine. Just leave me alone. I'll go to seminary." I left the high school after only one year of teaching, and I got a glowing letter from the administration about how they'd never seen someone have such an impact after only one year, etc. That letter, while kind, was exactly what I didn't need. I already thought all of these incredible things happened because I was so gifted and so spiritually mature. Turns out there were a group of students who started interceding for their school in prayer their freshman year. By the time I came along they were seniors, and God poured out answers to their years of faithful petition. I stumbled in and thought I deserved the credit. Thinking back, it's embarrassing.

I did end up going to seminary, with my brother Mark, in Dubuque, Iowa. While we were there, we started a youth ministry. It was extremely successful. We were in a town that was 75-80% Catholic, but many of these Catholic kids were coming to our group. I thought, once again,

"I am the great anointed one. Everything I touch is blessed and turns to gold." You can imagine, then, that when we got out of seminary I had high expectations for the church I was going to start.

DISILLUSIONED

I graduated from seminary assured that I was talented, favored, and winsome. I was starting a church and I told my brother, "You're supposed to start it with me." I can still remember the conversation. I can see him giving me the eye, and of course he didn't want to start a church with me. Who would? I was arrogant and full of myself. I started a small church without Mark, and I thought it was the beginning of great things.

Two years went by, and it was not going so well. We had maybe 40 or 50 people in the church, and so little money came in that once we paid rent for the church there was nothing left over for me. I lived in my aunt's house, and by that time I was 33 years old. It was embarrassing to meet people I hadn't seen for a while. They'd tell me they had great jobs, they owned houses, their businesses were successful, etc. They'd invariably ask me, "What are you up to, Dave?" "Oh, I started a tiny church and I live with my aunt." I was humiliated, and I was doing everything in my power to make the church work. I was working 11-12 hours a day, and believe me, most people who say that aren't actually working that much. I was. I made phone calls, prayed, strategized, preached, and did everything I could think of, but it wasn't working

After ten years, I was still working at that pace, and it was still getting me nowhere. I was married at that point, so I had a flailing church, a marriage on the rocks, no money, long hours, and I was 40 years old. They had to rush me to the hospital at one point because my entire body, from the top of my head to the bottom of my toes, went numb. I couldn't feel a thing. I walked in there, and they did all kinds of tests. When it was over, the doctor sat on his little stool, rolled over to me, and asked, "Why are you so stressed out?" I thought to myself, "Well, doctor, I'm a Christian pastor, and I'm living in the grace and peace of God." I don't know what I told him, but I was thinking that my life wasn't lining up with this perfect peace I had heard so much about. I was stressed out beyond belief. Nothing was working.

I reached the point where I was exhausted, humiliated, and I felt like a failure. After ten years of tireless work, I wanted out. "God, let me leave this job. Let me go back to teaching. I love coaching, I love teaching high school. Just let me leave this pastoring stuff and I'll be happy." Despite it all, being in that place was good for me. I had to admit my failure. Admitting that my efforts weren't doing it and acknowledging my shortcomings brought me to a place where I realized what Jesus was saying in John 15:5, "Apart from Me you can do nothing."

LESSONS LEARNED

You see, our natural talents will only take us so far. Your own strength, mental toughness, ingenuity, personality, knowledge, and experience will only take you up to a certain point. No matter how talented you are, you are going to reach a place where you are out of your depth and you need God.

After ten years of being a pastor, God finally had me where He wanted me. I had always prayed, but my prayers changed. My prayers were desperate. I needed God, and I knew it. He had called me to be a pastor, and I couldn't do it on my own strength.

> *Whoever exalts himself shall be humbled; and whoever humbles himself shall be exalted.*
> —Matthew 23:12

I thought I was this great, talented, anointed preacher, when the truth of the matter was that I was full of pride, focused on myself, and I was a terrible stutterer (a great quality for someone who speaks for a living). Even if I had been as talented as I had thought I was, it wouldn't have been enough. It was only when I humbled myself and admitted my weaknesses, my need for God, that things began to change, first in my heart, then in our church.

My brother had been with me for a few years by this point, and all of a sudden we were working well together. I started asking what he was better at than me so that he could handle those things. I started asking how we could be most effective. I realized that I didn't have to be jealous of my brother. After a Sunday where he preached a good message, I didn't have to go and try to write a better one—it was good for me when he preached well! It would bring people into the church.

My whole perspective shifted radically when I admitted my weakness and asked for God's strength. Power is made perfect in weakness because God's resources are greater than our own. In the early days of our church, when I lived for people's praise, a man who was visiting came up to me and said, "Great sermon." I was thinking, "Yes, yes, I know. I'm gratified that you have been blessed by my message." Then he continued and told me, "You know, I was just so encouraged listening to you preach. I mean, if God can use *you*, then He can use anybody!"

At the time, it was not my proudest moment. Today, however, it is. If the whole world sees my inadequacies and then takes a look at what has been accomplished in our church and in our ministries, then they will say, "There must be something to this God thing. Maybe God can use me too." I am thankful for my weakness because God gets the glory, because I have to lean on His strength.

When I finally got this into my head, a lot of amazing things began to happen, and not the least incredible was that my stuttering went away. I had stuttered for 40 years, and it simply vanished. Gone. The church grew and our community has been greatly impacted for Christ, and you know what? I am not the great anointed one. That title belongs to Jesus, and He is able to work through anybody—even me. Even you.

This is the testimony of my life the last 25 years: From age 40 to 65, whenever I have admitted my weakness and inability to God and then waited on Him, I've done more than I ever thought was possible. I've been given wisdom, insight, and direction in times of need.

Admitting weakness releases God's strength.

> *Therefore I am well content with weaknesses, with insults, with distresses, with persecutions, with difficulties, for Christ's sake; for when I am weak, then I am strong.*
> —2 Corinthians 12:10

CHAPTER 8

How to Live Without Worry

Seek first His kingdom and His righteousness, and all these things will be added to you. So do not worry about tomorrow; for tomorrow will care for itself. Each day has enough trouble of its own.

—Matthew 6:33–34

A little girl was watching her mother prepare a roast for dinner. Her mother cut off the ends and then put the roast in the pot to cook. The little girl asked her, "Mommy, why did you cut the ends off?" "I don't really know why," the mother replied. "Maybe it helps the juices soak in. I learned it from watching my mother, so why don't you go ask her?" The little girl wanted to get to the bottom of it, so she ran off and found her grandmother, asking her the same question. Her grandmother replied, "I don't know why... My mother always did it that way. Maybe it helps it brown more evenly. You should go ask your great grandmother, since I learned from watching her." Frustrated with the lack of an answer, the little girl trudged off to find her great grandmother, who was at this point very old. She climbed up next to her and said, "Nana, why do Mother and Grandmother cut the ends off of the meat?" The little girl's great grandmother looked up and said, "I don't know why they do it. I used to have to cut off the ends because my pot was too small."

I like this story because it demonstrates how most people live their lives. They don't really know why they're doing what they're doing; they're just imitating others. They want to be happy, but they've never really sat down and thought, "What do I need to do to achieve my goal?" Advertisements seep into their thinking, rote persuades them to copy their neighbors, and they end up living without purpose or direction.

I hope you realize that as a Christian you have a purpose. God designed you as a work of art, but He also designed you with your own work to accomplish. It's hard to see if you don't have an understanding of the kingdom of God (if you'd like to learn more about the subject, I would recommend my brother Mark's book *On Earth as It Is in Heaven*), but believe me when I tell you that God doesn't make any mistakes, and you were designed. You have a purpose, and you can choose to walk in that purpose or to chase after all of the things the world tells you you've got to have.

After decades as a pastor, I've noticed that most of the disillusioned, unhappy people who end up in my office seeking counsel arrived there because they chased after what the world promised would bring them happiness. Success, money, fame, and traveling are all fine as side-effects in life, but they make terrible idols. Seeking after our personal ambitions, courting the esteem of others, or hoarding as much wealth as we can in the end only causes us to worry constantly. For those who have not yet attained their goals, they worry that they never will; for those who have gotten all that they wanted, they worry that they will lose it.

Jesus tells us a different way.

> *For this reason I say to you, do not be worried about your life, as to what you will eat or what you will drink; nor for your body, as to what you will put on. Is not life more than food, and the body more than clothing? Look at the birds of the air, that they do not sow, nor reap nor*

gather into barns, and yet your heavenly Father feeds them. Are you not worth much more than they? And who of you by being worried can add a single hour to his life? And why are you worried about clothing? Observe how the lilies of the field grow; they do not toil nor do they spin, yet I say to you that not even Solomon in all his glory clothed himself like one of these. But if God so clothes the grass of the field, which is alive today and tomorrow is thrown into the furnace, will He not much more clothe you? You of little faith! Do not worry then, saying "What will we eat?" or "What will we drink?" or "What will we wear for clothing?" For the Gentiles eagerly seek all these things; for your heavenly Father knows that you need all these things. But seek first His kingdom and His righteousness, and all these things will be added to you. So do not worry about tomorrow; for tomorrow will care for itself. Each day has enough trouble of its own."

—Matthew 6:25–34

There is a lot to unpack in this passage, so we're going to break it up into four major instructions that Jesus has for us to live by. Before continuing, I encourage you to read the passage one more time and really let it sink in.

WORRYING IS USELESS

There are plenty of things that you and I are (and ought to be) concerned with at any given time. We have to take care of our families, work on our marriages, pay the bills, monitor our physical health, etc. None of these are problematic in and of themselves. Jesus is not telling you, "Don't plan." He's telling you, "Don't worry." What is the difference?

Planning is taking a look at what you have, what you need, and figuring out the best way to get from A to B. Worrying is being fixated on the bad things might happen in any given situation.

To live without planning is not more spiritual than planning for the future. As a matter of fact, if you fail to plan, you're in for a rude awakening at some point. What Jesus wants to tell us here is that we should not allow ourselves to be consumed by all of the potential bad that might come. Let me give you an example.

About a year ago, I went outside and noticed cracks in my pool. That might not sound so bad, but I live on top of a big hill. When the house was built, it took a hundred dump trucks of earth to build the pad underneath, so all of that is just fill dirt. When I saw the cracks, I thought, "Oh my gosh! My pool is going to break, half of the hill is going to wash away, the foundation will be compromised, and then it will collapse!" All of these thoughts came to me in about 20 seconds. I brought a pool guy over who looked at the cracks and said, "Don't worry about it. Most pools crack. Those are no problem."

Worry is exhausting. I needed to call in an expert to get his opinion on the cracks in the pool, sure, but I didn't need to freak out about it. Fundamentally, we worry over things outside of our control. We worry that at the crucial moment we won't have enough money, we won't have enough resources, we won't have the talent, etc. When there is a problem (or a potential problem) that we can't fix, our minds naturally tend to dwell on negative scenarios. I've heard someone sarcastically shout, "I can't do anything about it, but at least I can worry!" As if that helps anything.

Corrie ten Boom, a Christian woman who lived during the Nazi occupation of the Netherlands and a concentration camp survivor, said,

"Worry doesn't empty tomorrow of its sorrow; it empties today of its strength."[5]

Science has connected worry and stress to heart problems, elevated blood pressure, ulcers, thyroid issues, headaches, and stomach disorders. It is literally, physically possible to be worried sick. Is it any wonder that Jesus asks us, "Who of you by worrying can add a single hour to his life?" Worry covers your thinking like a thick blanket of fog. You lose sleep, you're not able to perform at your job, you snap at your wife and kids, and you're distracted at church. All thoughts go back to the worry fog.

Let me ask you, does that sound like a helpful condition in which to make crucial decisions? No coach ever told a boxer on his way into the ring, "Tense up! I want you to go in there wound as tight as a drum. Be immobilized by tension. Flex every muscle in your body!" What do they actually say? "Loosen up. Float like a butterfly; sting like a bee." You can't fight your battles when you're consumed with fear.

The point is this: Jesus tells us that worry solves nothing. It doesn't soften the blow of future suffering—it amplifies it. Most of the time what we worry about doesn't even happen, so in that case the worrying was stress and strain for no reason. Even when what we fear does come about, all our worrying did was prolong the suffering. Worry robs us of joy and of strength, usually when we need them most. Jesus says worrying is useless, and we'd do well to listen to Him.

GOD KNOWS WHAT YOU NEED

The second thing Jesus emphasizes in this passage is that God already knows what your needs are. How could you be overlooked by

---

[5] Ten Boom, Corrie. Clippings From My Notebook. Thomas Nelson, June 1, 1982.

Someone who sees everything? God is omniscient (all-knowing). He created the universe. He sees you, and Scripture assures us of that fact.

> *For the ways of a man are before the eyes of the Lord and He watches all his paths.*
>
> —Proverbs 5:21

> *The eyes of the Lord are in every place, watching the evil and the good.*
>
> —Proverbs 15:3

> *There is no creature hidden from His sight, but all things are open and laid bare to the eyes of Him.*
>
> —Hebrews 4:13

In our humanity, we have this fear that says, "God sees everyone… except me. I've been overlooked." Impossible.

> *Great is our Lord and abundant in strength; His understanding is infinite.*
>
> —Psalm 147:5

We have to remember that nothing catches God unaware. Not only does He see everything that happens in your life but He cares too. He died for you.

> *Are not two sparrows sold for a cent? And yet not one of them will fall to the ground apart from your Father. But the very hairs of your head are all numbered.*
>
> —Matthew 10:29–30

God knows what you need before you even ask Him.

SEEK GOD FIRST AND HE'LL PROVIDE

Imagine that you have volunteered to help an organization set up for a benefit in the evening. It's something you care a lot about, and so you want to see the event go well. You show up in the morning, meet the event coordinator, who tells you where all of the tables and chairs need to be set up. It's a few good hours of work. You ask about lunch, and the coordinator tells you there will be lunch provided for you later and not to worry about it, then she leaves. You work for a little while, but then you keep thinking about lunch. It's already 10:00, and you feel like you get low blood sugar when you don't eat. Besides, there are some foods you'd rather not eat, and you hadn't discussed it with the coordinator. Finally, you take a break from setting up to call the coordinator to ask for some details about lunch, but you can't get through. You call again, no answer. You try to start working again, but you're really concerned about lunch, so you stop and call a few friends to see if they can plan to bring you something. Everyone is busy. You get roped into a long conversation with your mother and she can't bring you food either. You've spent 40 minutes on the phone calling around without success. You decide to call the coordinator again, no answer. There's a lot of work to do, and if you can't count on your strength being kept up by food, how will it get done? You decide to see if there are any restaurants within walking distance, but your phone is on low battery. After a few minutes of searching, it dies, but you saw a fast food place three miles away—there's nothing closer. You don't want to eat fast food, but you're going to need to eat, so you walk around the site until you find other volunteers working on other projects, asking for a ride. No one can give you a ride, so finally you set out for the walk yourself.

It's hot, you sweat through your clothes—the clothes you planned on wearing for the benefit. You finally arrive at the fast food joint, and you order a hot dog and a coke, which costs more than you thought, and you sit down to eat it at the restaurant. It was either too greasy or too old, because as you're walking the three miles back to the site, it gives you a cramp. Upon your return, it's 2:30, nothing is set up, and there's too little time left for you to do it all yourself. Another volunteer walks up and says, "Where were you for lunch? The coordinator brought steak. Ruth's Chris catered for free."

What was the end result of your insistence to take care of lunch before taking care of your work for the benefit? You're tired, sweaty, sore, bloated from unhealthy food, and you missed out on a great lunch. Oh, and the work still isn't done, nor is there enough time now, so other people have to be pulled away from their work to do yours.

This isn't a perfect example, but I think it gives us a picture of what happens when we look to our own needs before seeking the kingdom of God: We miss the good that God has planned, we get something subpar, and the work either doesn't get done or it pulls a productive person away from his task.

Jesus promises us that God not only sees our needs but that if we look after the things of God first, God will provide for us. Lunch is already catered. Just because we don't know the plan doesn't mean it isn't happening.

When you examine the Greek word for "seek" in the passage we're discussing, you'll find that it's in the present imperative, which suggests a continuous action. It means "keep seeking." We have to continually seek God first every day because we forget. It's easy to become consumed with worries over our needs and desires. It's just so easy to let other things get in the way.

This is why so many mature Christians suggest that we spend devotional time with the Lord first thing in the morning. If we prioritize Him and His work, He will take care of us, and our perspective will be right. After all, isn't life more than chasing after our shifting needs?

And He died for all, so that they who live might no longer
live for themselves, but for Him who died and rose again

> *on their behalf... Therefore, if anyone is in Christ, he is*
> *a new creature; the old things passed away; behold new*
> *things have come.*
>
> —2 Corinthians 5:15, 17

A lot of people are familiar with 2 Corinthians 5:17, but fewer look at verse 15. Plenty of people talk about how Jesus' entrance into our lives makes us new creations and new possibilities open up, but it's tied to the fact that we aren't supposed to live for ourselves anymore. This is radical. It's anti-cultural. Our society is all about living for yourself— "Love yourself first," "Self-care," and "Follow your heart." The Bible tells us that we as Christians ought to be living not for ourselves but for Jesus.

The sad fact of the matter is that there are so many Christians out there who are miserable, sorrowful, confused, and depressed. Maybe you're one of them. Our default setting is to try out the world's way, to find our own solutions to our problems. We think that more money, another promotion, a bigger family, getting married, getting divorced, or more recognition will make us happy, but it won't. We can't live halfway. A man can't serve two masters. If we've given our lives to Jesus, what business do we have starting with our own needs?

> *Unless the Lord builds the house, they labor in vain who*
> *build it; unless the Lord guards the city, the watchman*
> *keeps awake in vain.*
>
> —Psalm 127:1

Our priorities need to be right in order for us to live well, and having right priorities means God's kingdom comes first. When we put God first, the Bible says that He'll guide us, provide for us, and that our steps will be established. Jesus is essentially telling us, "Focus on Me and not your problem. There might be some things you need to take care of to be responsible, but give it to Me, focus on Me, and I'll take care of it."

Let me give you one more illustration.

In 1910, a ship was sailing from London to New York, and the captain had brought his family with him. Three days into the journey they hit a terrible storm in the middle of the night, and the boat began rocking and tossing with the waves and wind. The captain's 8-year-old daughter woke up screaming and crying, terrified of the storm and the darkness. Her mother rushed in to her cabin, and the little girl asked, "What's going on?" The mother told her that they had hit a bad storm. The girl stopped and thought for a moment, then asked, "Is Daddy on deck?" Her mother told her that he was. The little girl stopped crying then, laid back down, and went to sleep.

Your Heavenly Father is on deck. You can have perfect confidence that He is steering you through the rough seas of life.

CONCENTRATE ON TODAY

You can't change the past and you don't know the future. The only time you can change things is today. I believe one of the strategies of Satan is to get Christians obsessing about what might happen tomorrow—as if we could be certain. Thinking this way causes us to load tomorrow's burdens on top of today's, which saps our strength and neutralizes our effectiveness for the kingdom of God. God gives us the strength we need for each day. You and I are not going to sink under the burden because God promises we will not, but tomorrow's concerns have the power to crush us. Leave them in the future where they belong, and when they come to you, God will give you strength for that day.

Have you ever come back from the grocery store with half a carload of bags and you decide that you only want to make one trip? How well does that usually go? Bananas fall out of one bag, the potatoes slip out, and by the time you've made it to the door, you've lost your keys and gained a hernia. If you have the patience to just take one load at a time, none of that happens.

Jesus is telling us to take one load at a time. You may have heard someone say it like this, "Life by the yard is hard, but by the inch it's a cinch."

Thinking this way radically changed my life. As our church grew over the years, there were needs for new skills and leadership popping up constantly. I was constantly expected to do things I was never trained for, and it seemed impossible at times. I learned early on that if I take each situation and just whittle away at it a little bit each day, that huge problem gets broken down into something manageable, something I can carry. By the inch, it's a cinch.

Living one day at a time will revolutionize your life.

A New Pattern

Learning to live this way takes an adjustment, but if you pray and seek God, He will help you do it. I have a prayer that I pray in some form every morning when I wake up, and I would encourage you to do the same:

> Dear Father, whatever comes this day, I give it to You. You are the way, the truth, and the life, and I know that You are the answer to whatever the enemy throws at me today. I'm going to live this day to the fullest to You, Lord. Help me to handle the unexpected things that arise with Your grace and mercy. Help me to see and accomplish Your work first today. Amen.

Matthew 6:25–34 is a manual for life, and I'd encourage you to memorize the whole thing. If that seems like too much, just start with verses 33-34. It will help to set your mind on God's way of tackling each day.

To sum up, Jesus tells us four things in this passage:

1. Worrying is useless. It does nothing for you but cause you stress and pain.

2. God knows what you need. He sees you.

3. Seek God first; He'll provide.

4. Concentrate on today. Let God handle the future.

When you can submit to these four truths and imperatives, you will find that the day is no longer overwhelming. God's mercies are new every morning.

> *Seek first His kingdom and His righteousness, and all these things will be added to you. So do not worry about tomorrow; for tomorrow will care for itself. Each day has enough trouble of its own.*
>
> —Matthew 6:33–34

CHAPTER 9

How to Endure

Let us hold fast the confession of our hope without wavering, for He who promised is faithful; and let us consider how to stimulate one another to love and good deeds, not forsaking our own assembling together, as is the habit of some, but encouraging one another; and all the more as you see the day drawing near.

—Hebrews 10:23–25

Take a journey with me back in time, over 3,000 years into the past. The place is Mt. Sinai in the wilderness of the Middle East, and you are an Israelite standing with your people listening to Moses, *the* Moses, telling you that God is going to come and visit in three days. He tells you that you have to go home to your tent and clean everything. Wash your clothes, wash your tent, and prepare yourself. Holy God will visit His people.

On the third day there is a blast from the trumpet, and you hurry to present yourself among the people in your best clothes, trying not to let your knees knock together. The earth begins shaking, smoke appears on top of the mountain. Fire comes down from the heavens, and thunder rends the skies. The shaking increases more and more until you can hardly take it, and you know that if you were any closer to the mountain you would die. Moses speaks, shouting into the noise, and

God answers with thunder. Then, God Himself comes down and rests on the top of Mt. Sinai.[6]

What a tremendous, life-defining, history-making experience. If I had a time machine, this is where I would go. Almighty God, the Unmoved Mover, the Creator and Sustainer of Heaven and Earth chose to come down in the sight of His people and speak to their chief. In this awesome and holy moment, God gave commands to His people, and the fourth thing He said was, *"Remember the Sabbath day, to keep it holy"* (Exodus 20:8).

What's more, in modern times, God has sent us the Holy Spirit, so what we have is even better than what the ancient Israelites had on that fateful day. Every Sunday we are invited to fellowship in the redeeming love, death-defying power, and holy rest of God with our brothers and sisters who are filled with His Spirit.

Bearing all of this in mind, this is what the devil will tell you at 7 a.m. on a Sunday morning: "It's not a big deal if you miss church. Watch the game."

How patently absurd.

God has given us a tremendous, monumental gift. We do not have to bear our burdens alone—we can go where Jesus is sure to be present, in the company of others who are supposed to love and encourage us.

Hebrews 10 tells us that we need to be certain not to fade away from attending church, and it puts it in the context of holding fast to our faith. Clearly, the Bible considers this to be an important issue, but where did it come from? Why does it matter what we do on Sunday morning each week?

---

[6] Exodus 19.

ORIGINS OF THE SABBATH

At the beginning, God created the heavens and the earth. It took Him six days, and on the seventh He rested. This is the first rationale we have for the Sabbath:

> *For in six days the Lord made the heavens and the earth, the sea and all that is in them, and rested on the seventh day; therefore the Lord blessed the sabbath day and made it holy.*
>
> —Exodus 20:11

We are to be imitators of God (Ephesians 5:1). God worked hard for six days and rested on the seventh, thus laying out the pattern for us to live by. The first purpose of the Sabbath is to take a break from your work once a week to let your body, mind, and spirit recover and rest. The Sabbath rest is like the moment of awed silence at the end of an incredible performance; it is the capstone that celebrates a good work accomplished.

God probably could have continued working on the seventh day, but in His kindness, He has given us a day of rest, and we need to accept that with thankfulness. This is only the first reason for the Sabbath, however, and we are going to spend most of this chapter discussing the second reason.

In Deuteronomy 5, the commandment is given and God tells Israel, just like in Exodus 20, that they need to let their servants and even their work animals rest. The text goes on to say:

> *You shall remember that you were a slave in the land of Egypt, and the Lord your God brought you out of there by a mighty hand and by an outstretched arm; therefore the Lord your God commanded you to observe the sabbath day.*
>
> —Deuteronomy 5:15

The Sabbath is not only a day of rest, but it is also a day to remember and refocus. When you walk into church each Sunday, more than likely you are immediately confronted with a cross. As Christians, we cannot look at that ancient instrument of torture without remembering Who bled on it. We were once slaves in our sin, we are sinners in need of a savior, and we have been redeemed and called to a greater purpose. Many a Sunday I come into the sanctuary beaten down from spending six days in the world, but I leave service refreshed and full of hope. We need to be reminded of who we are in Christ, and we need to be filled with hope and refreshing on a regular basis. God established the Sabbath, in part, so that we would remember what He has done for us. When we do, it changes everything.

OLD AND NEW TESTAMENT SABBATHS

In the Old Testament, it was very important that the Israelites observed this day of rest and remembrance on Saturday, as this was part of the ritual law setting Israel apart from the surrounding nations. In the New Testament, we observe that from the earliest times, Christians have observed this day on Sunday instead, in order to celebrate Christ's victory over death. We know this because of passages such as Acts 20:7.

> *On the first day of the week, when we were gathered to break bread, Paul began talking to them, intending to leave the next day, and he prolonged his message until midnight.*

The first day of the week is Sunday. 1 Corinthians 16:2 supports this also, as does the testimony of early church leaders such as Ignatius, who was born in 35 AD and writes of meeting with the brethren on Sundays.

Why is this significant? Two reasons:

One, it is important that we know how to honor God's commands, and taking our cue from the disciples, it becomes clear that celebrating the Sabbath on Sunday is a long-established and acceptable tradition.

Two, we can learn a lot from the order of things. In fact, it is revelatory when you grasp it. The Sabbath was celebrated on Saturday in the Old Testament, the time when God's people were under the law. Saturday is the last day of the week. It was necessary to toil all week before that rest and completion could be achieved. God's people lived in a condition of waiting for completion to come. Sunday is the first day of the week, as we said before. It is significant that God's people today, now under the law of Christ, begin with completion. Every week starts with rest, remembrance, and the assurance that all has been accomplished in Jesus' finished work on the cross. The kingdom of God, which is now here and yet still coming, expands out of that finished work. Our week begins in victory and spurs us onto our work, operating not in fleshly determination but from partaking of God's grace.

It is therefore very important that we understand why Sunday is generally our day of celebration, because we need to begin our endeavors in sonship, working out of it instead of for it. Each individual, however, is free to observe the Sabbath on another day if life circumstances force them to (Romans 14:5; Colossians 2:16). What matters most is that he or she assembles weekly with the church to rest and remember what God has done. Many churches have Saturday night services to accommodate people who have to work on Sundays—personally, I'm glad the police department doesn't take the day off, for instance. Some churches offer Friday services or even midweek meetings for those who work weekends. All of this is fine by the Scriptures as long as you observe the Sabbath with the assembly of God where you are.

Failing to attend church because of a medical emergency or having to celebrate on a different day due to work is one thing. Choosing not to attend because of a football game or a day at the beach is quite another. If we put our recreation and home improvement projects ahead of meeting together with God's people, we have transgressed the fourth commandment.

Consequences for Regularly Missing Church

But the children rebelled against Me; they did not walk in My statutes, nor were they careful to observe My ordinances, by which, if a man observes them, he will live; they profaned My sabbaths. So I resolved to pour out My wrath on them.

—Ezekiel 20:21

This is one of many, many such scriptures that show how seriously God takes His commandment that we observe the Sabbath. When Israel decided not to follow God's rules, there were consequences. There are consequences for us today, as well.

Failing to attend church regularly is often the start of sliding into spiritual dullness. All of a sudden, though you might well be saved, you aren't active or operating in God's power. You've been neutralized. From spiritual dullness often comes lukewarmness, and Jesus said that He will spit the lukewarm out of His mouth. A lukewarm Christian claims to follow Jesus but instead follows everything the world tells him to. He is a Christian in name only, and that is why the writer of Hebrews puts church attendance in the same breath as "hold[ing] fast the confession of our hope without wavering."

I like how my brother says it: We need to come to church and worship together and have hands laid on us regularly because we leak. Friend, this world will suck the truth of Jesus right out of you if you let it. We all need a weekly reminder of God's faithfulness, His sovereignty over our lives, and how important it is to obey Him, because the world is constantly trying to convince us otherwise.

I once read about a particularly relevant practice among miners from the old days. Miners digging deep into the mountains would take their pack mules all the way up the shaft, up the mountainside, and into the meadows to let them run around and play in the sun for a while. They would do this once a week, not because they had such an abiding love for their animals, but because if they didn't, the mules would actually go blind. Even in the physical world, we need a glimpse of light on a regular basis to keep from being overcome by the darkness.

Coming to church regularly is an act of submission to God's commands and an act of worship. We are supposed to gather and encourage each other, to prepare ourselves and each other for whatever life might throw at us next. If we continue to miss out on the opportunity to receive strength in the faith, then we will be unprepared for the storms of life. And make no mistake, storms will come.

WHY YOU SHOULD GO TO CHURCH

After people got saved in the cities that Paul visited, he established churches. The Church was Jesus' idea and He Himself is the founder. Jesus calls the Church His "bride." 1 John 3:14 tells us that one of the signs of salvation is that we "love the brethren." When you love somebody, you want to be around them!

The question of "Do you have to go to church to be a Christian?" is best answered with another question: "Why would a Christian not want to be a part of God's larger work in the community? Why would a Christian not want to go to church?"

The devil tries to tell people lies about their church attendance. He tells them that 1.) Nobody notices when they're not there and 2.) It doesn't matter if they go or not. Neither is true.

There is spiritual power in numbers, my friend. Deuteronomy 32:30 tells us that one can chase a thousand and two can chase ten thousand. Jesus tells us that wherever two or three are gathered in His name, He is there and present. Even if all you accomplish on a Sunday morning is to show up in good faith, that is good for the kingdom of God. Your presence, your talents, and your experience all make up a unique part of the Body of Christ. Can the body live with a few less fingers or toes? I suppose it could, but not one of you reading this would volunteer to lose a toe. The Church is better and more effective when every part of it is engaged, and a more effective church means more salvations, more baptisms, and a society that reflects Christ's love.

I don't have a scientific study on this, but from my experience and from speaking with many other pastors in our area, I can tell you that church attendance took a dip around 2012. Tithing stayed about the same, so what that tells me is a lot of people here in Southern California still love the Lord and still believe in contributing to the Church—they just stay home two or three weekends a month. It is interesting to note that when attendance started to drop off, the number of new salvations and baptisms declined as well. The two are certainly related.

Most Sunday mornings at most churches around the country see a good number of seats empty. Imagine that your church was filled beyond capacity, with people sitting on the floor and standing by the doors trying to hear the Word. I cannot imagine anything other than profound revival coming from that. Your presence matters as a witness to others—even when your kids are pulling each other's hair out and your tie's a mess, and your wife has half her make up on and one shoe as you pile into the car, your neighbors will think, "Man. They really are committed to getting to church each week." Your presence matters as an encouragement to others. You might see someone who is having a rough week, and you're in the right place to pray for them and give them some love and wisdom. This is why the passage in Hebrews talks about "stimulating one another to good deeds." Iron sharpens iron, my friend, and unless you want to grow dull, make church attendance part of your every week.

Some people have been hurt by members of the Church. I'm not excusing that. The Church is an institution made up of people. People are sometimes mean, bigoted, irresponsible, or misleading, and tremendous hurt can come from a church member or especially a pastor acting contrary to the teachings of Jesus. Some Christians have been left with a bitter taste in their mouth. As difficult as it may be to walk through such an experience, I'm here to tell you that now is the time to work it out, move past it, and rejoin your brothers and sisters in Christ. If you have been waiting for a sign from God, here it is. Go back to church. Get counseling if you need to. If the church is in error and preaching and practicing heresy, find a new church and be dedicated there. Do not let one hurt cause another in your heart. If we do not meet with the saints on a regular basis, we will grow dull.

I heard once about a preacher in a rural community made up mostly of farmers. He noticed after a few Sundays that it had been a while since the Shaw family had been in the pews, so he thought that he ought to pay Mr. Shaw a visit and see if everything was alright. The preacher saddled up his horse and rode out to the countryside, where Mr. Shaw was surprised to find him knocking at his door. The preacher was invited in, and as it was a cold winter's evening, they sat by the stove as they talked.

"To what do I owe the pleasure, Reverend?" Mr. Shaw asked.

"I noticed your family hasn't been to church in a while, and I wanted to make sure everyone was alright and see if there was anything we could do to help," the preacher replied.

"Oh, nothing's wrong, Preacher. It's just a busy time. There's a lot of work to do before the spring comes, and we have animals to take care of. Besides, it isn't as if one has to go to church to be a Christian," Mr. Shaw laughed.

The preacher, in response, merely nodded as he quietly rose and walked to the stove. He took a pair of tongs and reached into the fire, pulling out the brightest, hottest coal, and then he unceremoniously set it on the hearth, away from the flame. Mr. Shaw and the preacher sat in silence together, transfixed on the bright, burning ember that instantly began to cool and grow dull, until soon it was black, cold, and isolated on the stone.

"Reverend," Mr. Shaw began, breaking the silence, "this Sunday the Shaws will be in attendance."

> *Let us hold fast the confession of our hope without wavering, for He who promised is faithful; and let us consider how to stimulate one another to love and good deeds, not forsaking our own assembling together, as is the habit of some, but encouraging one another; and all the more as you see the day drawing near.*
>
> —Hebrews 10:23–25

CHAPTER 10

How to Fear God

The fear of the Lord is the beginning of knowledge.

—Proverbs 1:7

God said, "Let there be light," and there was light. Out of nothingness, He spoke the universe into existence. Every tree, rock, hill, plain, animal, scientific concept, star, galaxy, each of the billions of lives that have come and gone in history, and time itself, God created by speaking it aloud.

That is power.

The earth is just shy of 25,000 miles around at the equator. The sun is 2,720,984 miles around its equator—and our sun isn't even a very big star. A star called YV Canis Majoris is nearly 2 billion miles around. Both of these and a hundred billion more *that we know of* reside in a cosmos that is mostly made up by vast tracts of space. The diameter of the observable universe is calculated to be 5,500,000,000,000,000,00 0,000,000 miles. Just the diameter. It would take you four quintillion, five hundred quadrillion (4,500,000,000,000,000,000) *lifetimes* to walk that distance if you never stopped, rested, slept, or ate. God measured the universe with the length of His hand (Isaiah 40:12).

That is size.

God is not bound by time but sees all at once. God is not bound by space but can be (and is) present everywhere at once. God's attention is not limited. He is self-sustaining, and nothing else is. His ways are different and higher than ours (Isaiah 55:8–9). He doesn't sleep (Psalm 121:4), fail (Isaiah 55:11), or change (Hebrews 13:8). God is so holy that if a mortal man or woman were to see His face, that person would instantly die (Exodus 33:20).

Do you begin to grasp your inability to comprehend Him? What sort of Being are we talking about here? It boggles the mind.

God is love (1 John 4:8), and it is good that we talk about His grace and compassion for us. In the American church, however, there is very little discussion and a great deal of misunderstanding about the fear of the Lord. Our understanding, consequently, is wildly out of balance.

All too often, we hear people saying things like, "Well, sure the Bible says that it's wrong to cheat on my spouse/get drunk/tell lies/ hold onto a grudge/practice homosexuality/skip church/marry an unbeliever/ etc., but God and I have an understanding. It's complicated. It's ok for me to do this."

> *Can a man scoop fire into his lap without his clothes being burned?*
> —Proverbs 6:27 NIV

God is not someone to be trifled with. You do not have a special pass from God to insult Him by willfully sinning. Our culture is sorely lacking in the fear of God, which Proverbs tells us is the beginning of knowledge. If you want to be a Christian, you need to understand what it means to fear God.

FEAR DEFINED

I firmly believe that the fear of the Lord, after the message of the coming Messiah, is the most important theological concept in the Old Testament, and it is reaffirmed throughout the New Testament. Again and again we are told that blessings come when we fear the Lord. Again and again we see Israel suffer when they do not fear the Lord. In the books of the law, the wisdom scriptures, and in the prophets, we are instructed to fear God.

Most of the time, if you hear this idea talked about at all, preachers and commentators will say that the "fear" in fearing God really just means respect or reverence, like how you would rise if a dignitary came into the room. Some may sincerely believe this, and others might be trying to revise the Bible so they don't scare anyone away, but in either case, they are wrong.

Fear is not great respect. Fear means fear.

In the Old Testament, the Hebrew words "yare" (and its various forms) and "pachad" are translated as fear. In the New Testament, the Greek word "phobeo" (and its various forms) is used. These words mean "to frighten or terrify." The same word is used to describe one nation's terror of another's army (2 Kings 25:26; Jeremiah 41:18; etc.) and the fear of God and His law (2 Kings 17:25; Jeremiah 44:10; etc.). If the Holy Spirit had wanted Moses, Jeremiah, David, Isaiah, Paul, Matthew, and the other writers of Scripture to say "great respect," they would have used different words.

The Bible tells us to fear God, and it means it. In order to understand how, we first need a definition of fear and then a definition of the fear of God.

According to the Merriam-Webster Dictionary, "fear" means, "An unpleasant often strong emotion caused by anticipation or awareness of danger; anxious concern; profound reverence and awe; reasons for alarm."

According to my reading and studying, this is what the Bible basically means when it says the fear of God: "An understanding that there are consequences for disobedience and rewards for obedience."

People get confused sometimes because fear often comes along with other emotions. If you jump up on a stool when you see a spider, we can properly say that you are afraid of the consequences of crossing an arachnid. An agoraphobic (someone who's afraid to leave the house), by contrast, has a fear, but that fear is accompanied by ceaseless torment. Fearing God does *not* need to involve torment. Fearing God does *not* mean constant anxiety. The same Bible that tells us to fear God tells us not to be anxious (Philippians 4:6).

Fearing God means that you are afraid to defy Him. It means that you acknowledge that the world works the way that God says it does. You acknowledge and live according to the truth that sin will hurt you and faithfulness to God will prosper you.

THE PATH TO LIFE

In ancient Egypt, there was a pharaoh who looked upon the Hebrews living in his county and grew afraid. He saw how numerous they were, so he began to wonder what might happen to Egypt if they were to ever rise up and seize power. Not wanting this to happen, he enslaved the Hebrews, but their population continued to grow, which doubled his concern. We'll pick up the story in Exodus:

> *Then the king of Egypt spoke to the Hebrew midwives, one of whom was named Shiphrah and the other was named Puah; and he said, "When you are helping the Hebrew women to give birth and see them upon the birthstool, if*

it is a son, then you shall put him to death; but if it is a daughter, then she shall live." But the midwives feared God, and did not do as the king of Egypt had commanded them, but let the boys live. So the king of Egypt called for the midwives and said to them, "Why have you done this thing, and let the boys live?" The midwives said to Pharaoh, "Because the Hebrew women are not as the Egyptian women; for they are vigorous and give birth before the midwife can get to them." So God was good to the midwives, and the people multiplied, and became very mighty. Because the midwives feared God, He established households for them.

—Exodus 1:15–21

Here is the situation: Shiphrah and Puah were most likely the head midwives over quite a few others. The king of Egypt tells them to murder the males born to the Israelite women, and it's safe to assume that this wasn't just a casual suggestion. The king of Egypt had the power of life and death over these women, but even still, they knew that murder was against God's law. They feared God instead of the king of Egypt, and what happened? God blessed them.

Do not fear those who kill the body but are unable to kill the soul; but rather fear Him who is able to destroy both soul and body in hell.

—Matthew 10:28

Pharaoh was probably no dummy. When the midwives told him, "Gosh, the Hebrew women just keep giving birth to their boys every single time before we can get to them," I don't think he bought it. Yet somehow, he let them off the hook. They literally risked their lives because they feared God. *Do not miss this:* How easy would it have been for the midwives to say, "I'm no use to God if I'm dead. And Pharaoh is a harsh king, and he's threatening my life. Even though it is wrong, I have to do what he says, and God, in His mercy, will see my predicament and forgive me." Pharaoh only had the power to kill them; God would be judge of their souls. They rightly decided to throw in with God, knowing that by so doing they would be avoiding a worse fate.

God blessed the Hebrew women for fearing Him. Fearing the Lord always leads to life and blessing. Even if the king of Egypt had killed these women, they would have been blessed in heaven. Cheating death for a few years and then showing up before God in disgrace would have been a regrettable choice. But God chose to bless them in this life and shield them from the wrath of Pharaoh.

> *The fear of the Lord is a fountain of life, that one may avoid the snares of death.*
> —Proverbs 14:27

> *The fear of the Lord prolongs life, but the years of the wicked will be shortened.*
> —Proverbs 10:27

> *Behold, the eye of the Lord is on those who fear Him, on those who hope for His lovingkindness, to deliver their soul from death and to keep them alive in famine.*
> —Psalm 33:18–19

> *Fear the Lord, you His holy people, for those who fear Him lack nothing.*
> —Psalm 34:9 NIV

On the one hand, we must understand that defying God always leads to consequences. On the other hand, obeying God brings blessings. We have trouble with this concept sometimes because our perspective is limited. Let me give you an example:

If you've ever spent any time with a five-year-old, you know that they don't tend to be the most patient group. We ought to dress all vacationing five-year-olds in t-shirts that say "Are we there yet?" to save them the effort of asking it constantly. Imagine you have a five-year-old son who wants to write a letter to his technophobic grandmother, so you give him some paper and a stamp, and you explain to him how the post office works. He's enthralled by the magical concept of putting a letter in the mailbox and getting a response back, so he runs off and writes his letter, then sticks it in the mailbox. Five minutes later, he goes out to check the box. "It's still in there!" You tell him to wait; what you told him is going to happen. It just hasn't been long enough yet. He checks several more times that day, growing more and more disheartened, until when the mailman finally comes at three o'clock, it doesn't even excite him. "Finally," he thinks. Then, the next morning, he checks the mailbox and finds nothing. You try to tell him that he needs to wait, that his grandmother loves him and will certainly send him a letter back—but the letter probably hasn't even been delivered yet. Dejected, he doesn't believe you. He slumps and says, "It doesn't work. I'm never getting a letter back."

Cute, right? Slightly annoying, but cute. Kids have a warped perception of time, and if things don't happen instantly, they're suspicious at best, incredulous at worst.

Well, friend, you and I aren't much different.

"My coworker has been lying on his taxes, and the only consequence is a huge boat sitting in his driveway!"

"That con man skipped town! He got away with robbing me."

"Tom's been cheating on his wife for four years, and she has no idea. He has the family life and a little action on the side—and no one's the wiser."

"I tried to do the right thing by blowing the whistle on a dangerous product at work, and they fired me! That sure worked out well."

"I broke up with my boyfriend because he wasn't a Christian, and now I'm lonely. So much for God's promises."

If you've ever thought or said something like the exclamations above (and we all have), I think God was standing there like the parent in our letter-mailing example saying, "Give it a second. It's going to happen how I told you."

Sure enough, eventually our tax cheat gets audited by the IRS and that boat is a huge sign that says, "Send me to prison." Eventually the police will nab the con man. Eventually Tom's wife will find out, he will probably get divorced, lose much of his financial security, and his kids will resent him. For those that did the right thing, the whistleblower will get a new job that doesn't stab at his conscience (and will avoid repercussions when the market discovers the negligence) and the person who broke up with her non-believing boyfriend will most likely get another boyfriend, one who loves God and will make a good husband and father.

Fearing God is the path to life. Give it a second.

> *But if you will not do so, behold, you have sinned against the Lord, and be sure your sin will find you out.*
> —Numbers 32:23

> *Because the sentence against an evil deed is not executed quickly, therefore the hearts of the sons of men among them are given fully to do evil.*
> Ecclesiastes 8:11

FEARING GOD CONVICTS SINNERS

You've heard the song *Amazing Grace,* haven't you? It seems like everyone has; it's been one of the most universal and influential songs written in all of modernity. What you might not know is that the man who wrote it, John Newton, was an absolute degenerate for most of his life. He was a drunkard, sexually depraved, and a slave-trader. He lived for the quick dollar and immediate pleasures, but then one day he found himself aboard a ship that was threatening to sink in a terrible storm. The storm's fury was so bad, and John Newton's excesses so well-known, that the captain of the ship actually suggested that they consider throwing Newton overboard to appease God's wrath and end the storm. Newton found himself in fear for his life, realizing that within minutes he could die and have to answer for all of his sins before God. He knew that as he was, he would be sentenced to Hell.

That fear led to repentance. He got down on his knees and accepted Christ, begged forgiveness for his sins, and he began to live for the Lord. It was this experience that allowed him to write the part of *Amazing Grace* that says, "Twas grace that taught my heart to fear, and grace my fears relieved." God's grace—His love, His mercy, His unmerited favor upon us—taught Newton to fear the consequences of defying God. Then, when he was reconciled, that same grace removed the torment from him as a child of God.

The fear of the Lord is a good thing.

When I was 25 years old, I attended a worship service up in Anaheim, California. I had been a Christian for a couple of years, but there was compromise in my life. As I stood worshiping God at this wonderful church that day, raising my hands and singing with terrific music, I heard the Spirit of God tell me very clearly, "If you continue in this compromise, you will suffer consequences." My eyes popped open, and in the middle of the crowd, during a song, I actually said out loud, "Consequences?!"

You see, I had walked away from the Lord at 14, and I paid dearly for it. The Lord literally saved my life, and I had spent the three years prior to that moment at the church in Anaheim getting my mind back after I had fried it with drugs and paranoia. I knew right then what I had to do, and I went and did it at the first opportunity. I cut that compromise out of my life because I was scared of the consequences. I had had enough of consequences! I knew that I didn't need any more.

THE BEGINNING

Are there more reasons for following God's laws than a dread of negative consequences? Of course there are. What we have to understand, however, is that this deeper understanding can only come to us *after* we have fear of the consequences. The mark of a Christian is obedience to Jesus, and that obedience can certainly come from fear at first. As we grow in relationship with God, we will learn more about His ways, come to love Him in a deeper way, and our desires will change so that we want to obey Him for positive reasons as well. Fear of the Lord is the beginning of all of this.

Unfortunately, I have seen many people drift away from the Lord. I've seen pastors mess around on their wives, young people get mixed up in addiction—you name it, I've probably seen it. How can it be possible that people who say they love the Lord and live among His people for years can turn their backs on Him? I believe it is because they did not start with the fear of the Lord. When small compromises came calling (skipping prayer time, missing church to sleep in, flirting a little bit here and there with co-workers, etc.), they thought they were no serious matter. A thousand small steps later, they're way off track. No one wakes up in the middle of a great time with the Lord and says, "You know what I'll do today? I'll have an affair and wreck my life!" What a great many people do, however, is essentially say, "God doesn't care that I read *Cosmo* and watch scandalous soap operas every day while never picking up the Bible. He loves me, right?" Later they say, "Everybody flirts." Later it's "It's not a big deal. Men and women can be friends. We're an egalitarian society. It isn't going anywhere." Later it's "My husband/wife doesn't need to know." Inevitably, it ends with "How did everything get so messed up?"

Matthew 7 gives us a sobering warning:

Not everyone who says to me, "Lord, Lord," will enter the kingdom of heaven, but he who does the will of My Father who is in heaven will enter. Many will say to Me on that day, "Lord, Lord, did we not prophesy in Your name, and in Your name cast out demons, and in Your name perform many miracles?" And then I will declare to them, "I never knew you, 'Depart from Me, you who practice lawlessness.'"

—Matthew 7:21–23

This passage brings up a number of questions, but the main point I want you to take a look at is this: There will be people who have performed miracles who do not enter the kingdom of heaven. That should make us reconsider our flippancy with God's law. That should fill us with holy fear when the devil tries to tell us, "It's not a big deal," or tries to get us to make small compromises that rationalize our desires against God's Word.

The devil will try to get you to disregard God's Word, but if he doesn't succeed in that, he may try and make you feel tormented by the thought of, "What if I do [some terrible thing]?" Thankfully, God has given us free will. If you are afraid to defy God's law—then don't! And don't let the devil torment you with anxiety. Fear God and obey Him.

A SANCTUARY

I don't want you to take the wrong message away from this chapter. God is full of mercy and love and goodness. He is not waiting to smack you with a big stick if you mess up. However, defy Him at your own risk. People who compromise God's Word and sin against Him pay a price for doing so. I'm not saying that they don't have salvation from faith, but there is always a penalty in this life for sin, just as there is always blessing for obedience to God.

As a pastor, I've seen people make decisions and then I've seen the results. I've seen spouses who won't forgive each other, Christians going into business with unbelievers or marrying unbelievers, Christians holding onto bitterness and anger, habitually viewing pornography, robbing God of His tithe, etc. I've heard every rationale you can fathom: "The apostle Paul was just a product of his culture," "This passage isn't for today," "My situation is special, so the Bible doesn't apply," etc. The results of these rationales have been bad marriages, loneliness, demonic oppression, disease, bankruptcy, addiction, broken relationships, and, saddest of all, people missing out on what God has for their lives.

If you have messed up your life and taken a dark path, I have good news for you: Jesus can mend every wound, His sacrifice can cover every sin, and His love can overcome any wrong if you come to Him. No matter how bad things have gotten, you can enter God's love and acceptance. The point of this chapter, however, is this: Why get there in the first place? Why let things get so bad? People always say, "If I knew then what I know now." Well, God is telling you now so you'll know now.

We harvest what we plant, we reap what we sow, and what goes around comes around. That's how it works. It isn't always instant, but that's how it works. The Bible urges us to fear God and depart from evil, both so that we can avoid bad things and so that we can live the abundant life here and now.

> *Do not be deceived, God is not mocked; for whatever a man sows, this he will also reap.*
>
> —Galatians 6:7

Wisdom is personified in Proverbs 1, and this is what she says:

Then they will call on me, but I will not answer; they will seek me diligently but they will not find me, because they hated knowledge and did not choose the fear of the Lord. They would not accept my counsel, they spurned all my reproof. So they shall eat of the fruit of their own way and be satiated with their own devices. For the waywardness of the naïve will kill them, and the complacency of fools will destroy them.

—Proverbs 1:28–32

Fearing the Lord is the beginning, and it leads to good places. Choose the blessing and not the curse, and hear what the prophet Isaiah says:

It is the Lord of hosts whom you should regard as holy. And He shall be your fear, and He shall be your dread. Then He shall become a sanctuary.

—Isaiah 8:13–14

A sanctuary is a safe place, a place of refuge, a shelter from harm. If you fear the Lord and trust that obeying Him leads to blessing as surely as disobeying Him leads to pain, then God will become your fortress.

TWO KEY IDEAS TO REMEMBER

1. Fearing the Lord is a choice we must make every single day.

2. Don't let the devil fool you; there are always consequences for sin and blessings for righteousness.

God is a Being beyond our wildest imaginations. He spoke the universe into existence, and He decided the laws according to which it would run. The world operates how God says it does. When He says this leads to blessing and this leads to curses, He is right.

Fear God, depart from evil, and you will begin to understand.

The fear of the Lord is the beginning of knowledge.
—Proverbs 1:7

CHAPTER 11

How to Honor God with Your Finances

---

*Honor the Lord from your wealth and from the first of
all your produce; so your barns will be filled with plenty
and your vats will overflow with new wine.*

—Proverbs 3:9–10

My absolute favorite place on the planet to visit is Israel. I've been so many times that I've begun to lose track—somewhere between 12 and 15 trips. When I go to Israel, I'm always fascinated by the Dead Sea, which is a body of water that receives a constant inflow from the Jordan and a few other rivers, but there is no outlet. As a result, whatever water comes in just sits there. The soil under the Dead Sea has a tremendous mineral content, and the stagnant water leeches it out over time so that nothing can live in the water. When you go to swim in the Dead Sea as a happy-go-lucky tourist, the signs warning you to seek immediate medical attention if you get any of the water in your mouth, eyes, or ears sober you quite a bit.

Here's the interesting part: If there was a river flowing out from it, the Dead Sea would be alive. Fish and crustaceans and every kind of sea-dwelling creature could enliven the waters if only something would flow out of it.

It's the same with you and me. We stagnate when we only ever receive and never give.

THE BIBLE AND MONEY

In Luke 3, John the Baptist is preaching the gospel, and people come to him in response, saying, "What shall we do?" (verse 10). His answer is to share food and clothes with the poor (verse 11), for tax collectors to collect no more than is right (verses 12–13), and for soldiers to be content with their wages, extorting nothing (verse 14).

A crowd comes to the greatest prophet and asks what they ought to do after hearing the gospel, and the three things John says all have to do with money.

The word "love" appears in 309 verses in the Bible. The word "give" shows up in 876.[7] A large proportion of Jesus' parables are about money and possessions. The Bible talks about finances quite a bit, and it's important that we ask ourselves why.

This is a difficult subject to talk about in America because a lot of people conjure up images of charlatan televangelists raising money to buy private jets. The last time I preached on what the Bible has to say about money, the moment I opened my mouth some people got up and walked out. This is a touchy subject for many, but since the Word of God gives it so much time, we ought to understand and apply what God has in mind. My salary doesn't go up one iota if I convince a hundred or a thousand more people to start tithing. I teach on this subject because I want people to know what God says about handling their money so they may be blessed.

Why is money so important? Because the way we use our resources is central to our relationship with God. John the Baptist talked about money and possessions with his acolytes because he knew that he could not talk about life commitment to God to a people who would not commit their possessions to Him.

---

[7] From a search of the NASB, using an interlinear indexing that draws from *Strong's Concordance.* http://www.biblestudytools.com/interlinear-bible

Where your treasure is, there your heart will be also.
—Matthew 6:21

Money reveals our priorities in a way that few other things do. As Martin Luther supposedly said, "There are three conversions a person needs to experience: The conversion of the head, the conversion of the heart, and the conversion of the pocketbook." People say "put your money where your mouth is" for a reason.

Zacchaeus from the Bible provides us with a good example.

In Luke 19 we meet Zacchaeus, a tax collector. The Jews at this time in history despised tax collectors for a number of reasons, but most relevant to our discussion is because they often levied more taxes than were actually owed. When Zacchaeus met Jesus, his heart changed.

> *Zacchaeus stood up and said to the Lord, "Look, Lord! Here and now I give half of my possessions to the poor, and if I have cheated anybody out of anything, I will pay back four times the amount." Jesus said to him, "Today salvation has come to this house, because this man, too, is a son of Abraham."*
> —Luke 19:8–9 NIV

It is easy to hold up our hands on a Sunday morning and sing along with songs that say things like, "Lord, I give You my life," and, "I will follow You, God!" but if that doesn't translate into our lives, what does it mean? Isn't faith without works dead (James 2)? Jesus could plainly see that something had changed in Zacchaeus because he was willing to give of his finances. He was no longer trusting in money; he was fearing God.

I believe that the Bible's teachings on money can boil down to three key truths. If you understand and abide by these financial pillars, you will be blessed and God will be glorified in your finances.

1. Tithe

> *Thus all of the tithe of the land, of the seed of the land*
> *or of the fruit of the tree, is the Lord's; it is holy to the*
> *Lord... For every tenth part of herd or flock, whatever*
> *passes under the rod, the tenth one shall be holy to the*
> *Lord.*
>
> —Leviticus 27:30, 32

Very few things are called "holy to the Lord" in the Bible, but when speaking of the tithe, Scripture makes it clear that it is God's special possession. "Tithe" is simply an old word that means "tenth." One tenth of your increase belongs to the Lord. For a farmer or rancher living in ancient Israel, that means that if ten of your goats give birth to kids, one of those new goats belongs to God. If a hundred pounds of figs is harvested, ten pounds of it belongs to God. The tithe was used to take care of the Levites, the priests of Israel.

There is no real disagreement over what this practice looked like in the Old Testament. Where there is suddenly intense disagreement, however, is whether or not this practice applies to us today. After all, we don't worry about whether or not we're wearing mixed fabrics, and we don't have to feel bad about eating bacon. So we don't have to tithe, right?

Wrong.

Look at what Jesus says:

> *Do not think that I came to abolish the Law or the*
> *Prophets; I did not come to abolish but to fulfill. For*
> *truly I say to you, until heaven and earth pass away, not*
> *the smallest letter or stroke shall pass from the Law until*
> *all is accomplished. Whoever then annuls one of the*
> *least of these commandments, and teaches others to do*
> *the same, shall be called least in the kingdom of heaven;*

but whoever keeps and teaches them, he shall be called
great in the kingdom of heaven. For I say to you that
unless your righteousness surpasses that of the scribes
and Pharisees, you will not enter the kingdom of heaven.

—Matthew 5:17–20

Don't miss this: Jesus says that as New Testament believers our righteousness ought to exceed that of the Old Testament believer. Why? Because we have God's Holy Spirit living inside of us. In the Old Testament, prophets and mighty men of God would have the Holy Spirit come upon them. We have been given the Holy Spirit to dwell within us. What the prophets and mighty men of old experienced only once in a while, you and I can experience every day. Our resources are endless since the outpouring at Pentecost.

This is why Jesus raised the bar, so to speak, when speaking about Old Testament commands.

You have heard that the ancients were told, "You shall not
commit murder" and "Whoever commits murder shall
be liable to the court." But I say to you that everyone
who is angry with his brother shall be guilty before the
court... You have heard that it was said, "You shall not
commit adultery"; but I say to you that everyone who
looks at a woman with lust for her has already committed
adultery with her in his heart."

—Matthew 5:21–22, 27–28

Jesus is holding us to a higher standard. Yes, we are under grace, but we are told that if we love God we will follow His commands (John 14:15). "But Dave!" people complain, "I'm under a new and better covenant. The Old Testament rules don't apply to me anymore." A lot of people fall into this trap of thinking that they are beyond tithing as New Testament believers, and ultimately this stems from a misunderstanding of the biblical concepts of "milk" and "meat."

*Like newborn babies, long for the pure milk of the word,
so that by it you may grow in respect to salvation, if you
have tasted the kindness of the Lord.*

—1 Peter 2:2–3

*For though by this time you ought to be teachers, you
have need again for someone to teach you the elementary
principles of the oracles of God, and you have come
to need milk and not solid food. For everyone who
partakes only of milk is not accustomed to the word of
righteousness, for he is an infant. But solid food is for
the mature, who because of practice have their senses
to discern good and evil.*

—Hebrews 5:12–14

Tithing is milk. It is an elementary principle of godly living. Today, in light of the revelation given to us by Jesus, we know that tithing is not the end. Tithing is to teach us generosity. Generosity, the freedom to give without placing a maximum limit, is spiritual meat. So if you tell me that you aren't under the law and you don't believe in tithing, my response will be, "Praise the Lord! You've realized that you are free to give 15%, 25%, or even more to the Lord and His work!" People look at me funny when I say that, because of course that isn't what they meant. What they meant was, "I don't have to pay anything to the Church."

But does that make sense? If tithing is the elementary principle, how is the fulfillment of that concept miserliness? How is giving less than ten percent raising the bar for the modern believer who lives in the Spirit?

It's like all of those New Age gurus who say that they have progressed beyond the bounds of morality. But how can the step "beyond" morality be immorality? How can the promiscuity, fraud, and blatant dishonesty that inevitably follows from such a proclamation be the logical next step after chastity, justice, and honesty? Morality did not teach these people to be immoral; they simply rejected the foundational teaching.

People who go around teaching that you don't need to tithe, and who don't tithe themselves, have not learned to do so from the elementary principles of God's Word; they have rejected them.

Jesus tells us to "Render to Caesar the things that are Caesar's; and to God the things that are God's" (Matthew 22:21). The application of this teaching extends to every area of our lives, but it is important to remember that Jesus was asked specifically about money. (And what part of your money has God called holy to Himself? A tithe of your increase or income.)

The deeper into these issues that you go, the more it ought to become plain to you that every Christian ought to tithe to the local church. God, in His wisdom, has mandated it. The freedom that comes with being under grace means that you can now trust God with all of your finances and thus give beyond the minimum.

There are consequences for denying this, but there are also blessings for acknowledging and following it.

> *"From the days of your fathers you have turned aside from My statutes and have not kept them. Return to Me, and I will return to you," says the Lord of hosts. "But you say, 'How shall we return?' Will a man rob God? Yet you are robbing Me! But you say, 'How have we robbed You?' In tithes and offerings. You are cursed with a curse, for you are robbing Me, the whole nation of you! Bring the whole tithe into the storehouse, so that there may be food in My house, and test Me now in this," says the Lord of hosts, "if I will not open for you the windows of heaven and pour out for you a blessing until it overflows. Then I will rebuke the devourer for you, so that it will not destroy the fruits of the ground; nor will your vine in the field cast its grapes," says the Lord*

> *of hosts. "All the nations will call you blessed, for you*
> *shall be a delightful land," says the Lord of hosts.*
>
> —Malachi 3:7–12

The prophet Malachi basically tells us four things in this passage:

1. If you're not tithing, you're robbing God (v. 8).

2. If you're not tithing, your finances are under a curse (v. 9,11).

What is this curse? It is that God will not rebuke the devourer (Satan) from your finances. God has called ten percent of your increase holy unto Himself, and He isn't going to let you spend that ten percent. It will get eaten up, and the devourer will not stop at ten percent.

3. Bring the tithe into the storehouse (v. 10).

In the Old Testament, the storehouse was the Temple. Today, it is the local church, by which the surrounding community is blessed. Jesus established the Church as the focal point of His work on earth, and we need to support it.

4. If we tithe, we will be blessed (v. 10).

God is telling us to trust Him. We will be better off on 90% than on 100%. It isn't always immediate—I'm not going to sit here and tell you that if you give $50 today you'll get $100 back tomorrow—but over the years, you will be better off than if you had not given to the Lord what He has called His own.

2. Be a Good Steward

A "steward" is someone who directs the resources of another. God calls us to be good stewards of what He has given us, and in order to do this, we have to understand two foundational truths:

A. Everything Belongs to God.

The earth is the Lord's, and all it contains, the world,
and those who dwell in it.

—Psalm 24:1

"The silver is Mine and the gold is Mine," declares the
Lord of hosts.

—Haggai 2:8

Yours, O Lord, is the greatness and the power and the
glory and the victory and the majesty, indeed everything
that is in the heavens and the earth; Yours is the dominion,
O Lord, and You exalt Yourself as head over all.

—1 Chronicles 29:11

God created everything. He is the Originator, the Source, the Owner of the Land, the Maker, the Patent-holder, the Inventor, and the King. It's all His. You and I will always struggle with being obedient in our finances until we concede that God owns everything. Until we admit this, there will always be hesitation in obeying because we will fear that there won't be enough left for us, that God won't come through.

If God is really in control of everything (and He is), then He will supply the needs of His children.

B. You Are a Manager.

He who is faithful in a very little thing is faithful also in
much; and he who is unrighteous in a very little thing
is unrighteous also in much. Therefore if you have not
been faithful in the use of unrighteous wealth, who will
entrust the true riches to you?

—Luke 16:10–11

You and I have to be good managers with what God has given us. If we're honest with ourselves, most of the stress and anxiety we have experienced over our finances comes from being mediocre managers. I've certainly been there. I remember sitting at the kitchen table years ago and opening the credit card statement. I nearly had a heart attack. My wife and I had gotten into the habit of saying, "Well, the kids need something. Swipe the card," or, "The car needs gas. Swipe the card." It isn't that we were going out and buying vacations to Bora Bora and going on Gucci shopping sprees, we just weren't budgeting properly. A manager needs to put everything in its proper place.

If you are having trouble managing your finances, I would encourage you to look into a course by Dave Ramsey called *Financial Freedom*. I would also encourage you to pick up a book called *Our Giving Story* by Mike LaBahn.

In the grand scheme of things, money isn't the most important thing. If we can't behave responsibly even with that, however, then how is God to entrust us with managing true riches? True riches are spiritual gifts. How we manage our money is a test. If we do well with our first responsibilities, God will give us greater responsibilities. We can learn self-control, delayed gratification, generosity, resisting temptation, and faithfulness all from how we spend our money.

3. Be Generous

Generosity does not spring into existence from nothing. Usually it flows from first tithing and being a good manager with what you have. We learn from reading James 3:14-16 that selfishness (the opposite of generosity) is darkness, is evil, and we can see the destruction it creates in people's lives. Selfishness is the idea that I have to hold onto as much as I can because I might not have enough later. It doesn't end with being stingy, either. Usually a selfish person ends up lying, cheating, manipulating, distorting, or even stealing in order to keep his or her stuff. This sort of living will never lead you into God's will. Being generous, on the other hand, involves letting go, giving, and trusting God.

The word "give" is mentioned in the Bible nearly twice as often as "believe," "prayer," and "love" combined.[8] It is mentioned so often because it is critical to the condition of our hearts. A Christian's generosity is almost always a reflection of their faith and trust in God.

The question for you is this: Do you believe what God's Word says about giving? The Bible tells us again and again that if you give you will be blessed.

> *Give, and it will be given to you. They will pour into your lap a good measure—pressed down, shaken together, and running over. For by your standard of measure it will be measured to you in return.*
>
> —Luke 6:38

> *He who is generous will be blessed.*
>
> —Proverbs 22:9

Giving releases a spiritual dynamic, and it isn't just money. If you give love, you will find it. If you give mercy, you will receive it. If you forgive, you will be forgiven. It's almost like when we give, we enter into God's economy, and this economy has different rules than Wall Street.

In 2 Corinthians 9, Paul wants to make sure that you and I understand that when we give we are planting seeds. His point is that when you plant seeds, you aren't losing out. You are investing. The farmer doesn't go broke because he planted seeds; a harvest comes, and then he has more seeds to plant again.

---

8   Ibid.

I don't think it's a one-to-one ratio, and sometimes you might give money and receive a different kind of blessing in return. If you need a blessing in your marriage or with your kids, you would rather have that than more money. The important thing is that we take God at His word when He tells us to give, when He tells us how the world works, and in everything. There's good news with all of this: Obedient, generous Christians reap the blessings of God.

Remember the Dead Sea we talked about at the beginning of this chapter? The world tries to tell us that if we hoard more and more then we will be happy, but in reality we'd just end up like the Dead Sea, stagnant and unable to sustain life. If we have a river flowing out of us, however, then we can thrive and be a blessing to the world around us.

I'll end this chapter with a challenge. Will you take God's word for it? Will you trust what He says about tithing, managing, and generosity? If you do, you will be better off in more ways than one.

> *Honor the Lord from your wealth and from the first of all your produce; so your barns will be filled with plenty and your vats will overflow with new wine.*
> —Proverbs 3:9–10

Chapter 12

How to Live in the Power of God

For John baptized with water, but you will be baptized
with the Holy Spirit not many days from now.

—Acts 1:5

On a day-to-day basis, what makes you different from all of those
who don't follow Jesus? You've been given a moral code, certainly.
You have eternal hope and hope for the present. You have a sense of
belonging to a Body that is larger and greater than yourself, but also the
security of knowing that you have a special place inside of it.

The list can go on, but there is one thing that God specifically
promised His people. It is a gift that makes Christians different from the
rest of the world, a gift that is invaluable and yet is often disregarded,
forgotten, or abandoned. It is the difference between victory and defeat,
clarity and confusion, love and pride, confidence and insecurity. This
gift, long ago promised to God's people, is the Holy Spirit.

Have you ever been part of a church that seemed to be without
power, without effectiveness? You can have good theology, creative
programs, insightful teaching, and fashionable carpet in the sanctuary,
but where the Holy Spirit is missing, His power, guidance, and peace are
missing as well. I fear that in the American Church, there is a desperate
lack of humbly seeking after the Holy Spirit and a tremendous amount

of misunderstanding about what the Bible teaches concerning Him. Famed theologian A.W. Tozer put it this way:

> In most Christian churches the Spirit is entirely overlooked. Whether He is present or absent makes no real difference to anyone.... So completely do we ignore Him that it is only by courtesy that we can be called Trinitarian.[9]

I don't write this to be a naysayer or a Debbie Downer. This chapter is an impassioned exhortation to receive the fullness of what God has given to us, and it is also a stern warning to not miss out on what is helpful, necessary, and available for successful Christian living.

> *Apart from Me you can do nothing.*
>
> —John 15:5

Jesus tells us in John 15 that we need God to do anything! Anything of value, anything that runs contrary to the current of our culture, and any enduring work requires God's presence, power, and anointing. God promised to pour out His Spirit on all His people (Joel 2). Jesus told us He would send the Helper to us (John 16:7). Both promises have been fulfilled. It's raining with God's promises, but are you holding out your hands or covering your head?

Have you received the baptism of the Holy Spirit?

WHAT IS THE BAPTISM OF THE HOLY SPIRIT?

The baptism of the Holy Spirit is an impartation of God's power and anointing on a believer for daily sanctified living, administration of the spiritual gifts, and ability to accomplish God's work. Every

---

[9] Tozer, A.W. Chapter 5: "The Forgotten One" from *God's Pursuit of Man,* Moody Publishers.

believer receives the Holy Spirit at conversion, which is what we call "indwelling." Indwelling happens one time and only needs to happen one time. When you get saved, you've got the Holy Spirit living inside of you. As we see from the Bible, however, there is something else that can happen again and again, and that is what we call the baptism of the Holy Spirit: A refreshing, a renewing, an anointing, and an impartation of God's Spirit on you.

> *Now when the apostles in Jerusalem heard that Samaria had received the word of God, they sent them Peter and John, who came down and prayed for them that they might receive the Holy Spirit. For He had not yet fallen upon any of them; they had simply been baptized in the name of the Lord Jesus. Then they began laying their hands on them, and they were receiving the Holy Spirit.*
> —Acts 8:14–17

This is the picture we see in the New Testament (e.g. Acts 1:1-8; Acts 19:1-7): A person hears the Word of God, believes it, is baptized in the name of Jesus, receives the indwelling presence of the Holy Spirit, and is baptized in the Holy Spirit. A lot of people say that the indwelling at conversion is the same as the baptism of the Holy Spirit, but we know from the Gospels that this isn't true.

In John 20, the resurrected Christ breathes on His disciples and says, "Receive the Holy Spirit." At this point in history, Jesus had died for the sins of the world, conquered death, and in triumph He imparts the indwelling presence of the Holy Spirit to His disciples. I think we can safely say that when Jesus said to His followers "Receive the Holy Spirit" that they did in fact receive it right then. It would be odd, then, to consider this gift of the Holy Spirit at conversion the same as the baptism of the Holy Spirit, since Jesus tells these same disciples to not begin the work of evangelizing the world until they are baptized in the Holy Spirit:

> *Gathering them together, He commanded them not to leave Jerusalem, but to wait for what the Father had promised, "Which," He said, "you heard of from Me; for John baptized with water, but you will be baptized with the Holy Spirit not many days from now."*
>
> —Acts 1:4–5

Luke 24:49 says essentially the same thing. Jesus' prophecy was fulfilled shortly after, in Acts 2.

> *When the day of Pentecost had come, they were all together in one place. And suddenly there came from heaven a noise like a violent rushing wind, and it filled the whole house where they were sitting. And there appeared to them tongues as of fire distributing themselves, and they rested on each one of them. And they were all filled with the Holy Spirit and began to speak with other tongues, as the Spirit was giving them utterance.*
>
> —Acts 2:1–4

Not only do we see this clear distinction between receiving the Holy Spirit from Jesus in John 20 (indwelling) and being baptized in the Holy Spirit in Acts 2, but it happens to some of the disciples again in Acts 4.

The baptism of the Holy Spirit is not the same as salvation. Romans 10:9–10 tells us that anyone who confesses with his mouth that Jesus is Lord and believes in his heart that God raised Him from the dead is saved. Once we are saved and we have the Holy Spirit living inside of us, it is possible for the Holy Spirit to wash us in His presence and power, often to equip us to do a task that is beyond our ability or understanding.

Just look at what happened to the disciples. Once Pentecost happened and they were baptized in the Holy Spirit, everything changed. This baptism transformed these believers from timid fugitives to fearless, single-minded soldiers for Jesus. The power of God had fallen on them.

HOW DO WE KNOW THIS GIFT
IS FOR US AND FOR TODAY?

There is a group of people called cessationists who teach and believe that the gifts of the Holy Spirit are not for today. I'm not interested in attacking them because many cessationists are wonderful teachers and evangelists, and they are our brothers and sisters in Christ. When it comes to this issue, however, Scripture is clear. Paul tells us to earnestly desire the spiritual gifts (1 Corinthians 14:1), the disciples laid hands on new converts and prayed for them to be filled with the Holy Spirit (Acts 8; 19) which we sometimes see in the text resulting in spiritual gifts. The disciples received the baptism of the Holy Spirit, as did many people they prayed for, and Paul tells Timothy to pass along what he has learned from Paul to others who can then teach it to others (2 Timothy 2:2). He's talking about more than just this one issue, but the point remains: The pattern we see in the New Testament is the disciples receiving from the Lord, then not only passing it on but passing it on with instructions for passage down through time.

There is no biblical evidence to believe that this was only a one-time dispensation and that God's spiritual gifts and the baptism of the Holy Spirit are not for today. Since we see it in the Bible, have seen it in our church (I've certainly seen it in my own life as well), and are told to desire the spiritual gifts, we can safely know that we have access to the same Holy Spirit Who came upon and filled the disciples.

There is still work to be done: unreached people groups who need the gospel, injustices such as human trafficking, abortion, and corruption-induced poverty in many places around the world, and in our own country a decadent culture with declining rates of church attendance, salvations, and a great amount of ridicule directed at God. Can we solve these problems on our own strength? Of course not. We need God's power, anointing, and direction. Thank the Lord that the baptism of the Holy Spirit is for today.

WHAT HAPPENS WHEN SOMEONE IS BAPTIZED IN THE HOLY SPIRIT?

When a person is baptized in the Holy Spirit, sometimes they begin speaking in tongues. Other times they cry, shake, fall over, or even begin to prophesy. I have had the gift of being baptized in the Spirit a number of times over the course of my life, and I have had strong physical and/or emotional responses during some of these occasions. If you were to ask me, however, what the most common outward sign of receiving the baptism of the Holy Spirit is, you may be surprised to hear me say "nothing."

Most of the time thunder does not bellow out from the heavens, visions do not dance before your eyes, uncontrollable sobbing does not overwhelm you. At least, this has been my experience. This is a crucial truth: The presence or absence of various outward signs does not negate or affirm the authenticity of an encounter with the Holy Spirit.

There are some well-meaning churches out there that say a person has only received the baptism of the Holy Spirit if they speak in tongues. 1 Corinthians tells us of many gifts, and nowhere does the Bible say that you have to speak in tongues in order to receive this anointing and empowering of God. I've taken 12 examples from the New Testament of the Holy Spirit baptizing people and I've examined the results. What I've found is that you cannot put God in a box. He is sovereign. He acts in whatever way He deems best. The Holy Spirit "falls on" people two of those times (Acts 10:44; 11:15), "comes on" people two of those times (Acts 1:8; 19:6), is "received" two of those times (Acts 8:17; 10:47), and people are "filled" with the Holy Spirit the other six times (Acts 2:2, 4; 4:8; 4:31; 9:17; 13:9; Luke 1:41, 67). The results? Sometimes preaching, sometimes witnessing, sometimes speaking in tongues, sometimes prophecy, and sometimes there is no direct manifestation given, leading me to believe that maybe there wasn't one; they were simply empowered for whatever work lay ahead of them.

What does all of this tell us? It is wrong to take any one experience or manifestation (like tongues) and use it as a measuring rod on whether or not someone has been baptized in the Holy Spirit. I've shaken, I've cried, I've fallen down, and as I said before, I've felt nothing at all.

On one occasion, about a year and a half after I got saved, I was attending a church where they had a special service for receiving the baptism of the Holy Spirit. They invited anyone who wanted to receive it to come forward, and I was right there at the front of the line getting prayer. I wanted anything that God had for me. People around me were getting instruction on how to start speaking in tongues, and I was hearing it around me, but I felt nothing. I went away from that night incredibly disappointed and discouraged. I even shed a few tears. I asked God, "What's wrong with me? Is there some sin I haven't confessed?" The amazing thing is, despite my discouragement, as I look back on my life, something changed that very night. Soon after, I started a concert ministry and was regularly preaching to hundreds of people at a time; other ministry opportunities arrived and had God's blessing upon them as well. The whole trajectory of my life changed.

The important thing is this: God clothes you in His power, with new understanding, and with anointing when you are baptized in the Holy Spirit, giving you the strength to live for Jesus every day. Often when you are doing the Lord's work and you need a breakthrough, the Holy Spirit will come upon you, giving you the ability to go beyond what you thought was possible.

How Do I Receive the Baptism of the Holy Spirit?

Now suppose one of you fathers is asked by his son for a fish; he will not give him a snake instead of a fish, will he? Or if he is asked for an egg, he will not give him a scorpion, will he? If you then, being evil, know how to give good gifts to your children, how much more will your heavenly Father give the Holy Spirit to those who ask Him?

—Luke 11:11–13

Jesus answers this question plainly: If you want the Holy Spirit, ask for it.

That's it. God isn't limited to you asking, of course; someone can lay hands on you and you receive it or you can be minding your own business and the Lord decides to send His Holy Spirit upon you. Jesus' words in Luke ought to be a great comfort to you, no matter what. He says that God will give the Holy Spirit to those who ask. Pretty incredible, isn't it? So why don't more Christians take advantage of this wonderful gift? I'm sure there are many reasons, but there is one in particular that I'd like to address.

You may say, "Ok, Dave, I understand that the Bible shows us the baptism of the Holy Spirit and that I ought to ask someone to lay hands on me and pray that I'd receive it. The only thing is… I've seen some weird stuff. There are some whackos out there, and I don't want to be one of them, lost in deception."

This hesitation is understandable. There is quite a bit of emotionalism, emotional pandering, unruly, unrighteous behavior (blamed on the Holy Spirit), and pure fakery masquerading as God's gift. There is certainly deception out there. God, however, has promised not to give you a snake if you ask for a fish, nor a scorpion if you ask for bread. The symbolic significance of this phrase is deeper than you may know. Snakes and scorpions represent demonic forces in the Bible, as well as lies. The fish and bread are both symbols of Jesus' provision. Jesus is telling us that if you ask Him humbly and sincerely for the Holy Spirit, He isn't going to send an evil force upon you. You aren't going to receive confusion instead of the Holy Spirit. God gives to those who ask this of Him. We can be confident, and we don't need to be afraid of being one of "those whackos."

Consider this: Jesus loves you. He died for you. He cares for you. He designed you. He wants you to overcome. He wants you to be filled with faith in the face of whatever stands before you. He wants you to have the supernatural strength to resist the enemy with all of his doubts and lies. He wants you to be empowered to do His work. If you ask your pastor or a brother/sister in Christ to lay hands on you and pray for you to receive the baptism of the Holy Spirit—even if you ask God alone in the privacy of your home—God is going to move. You might not shake or cry, speak in tongues or fall down, but God is going to move. The Bible says that God hears whatever we ask of Him when we pray according to His will and that we receive it. Open your hands to the Lord and humbly pray, "Lord, You are good. I acknowledge that You are God. I'm thankful that You hear me, and I need you. Fill me with Your Holy Spirit. I want more of You. Anoint me to speak to my coworkers about You/to pray for the sick/to know how to share about Jesus/to understand the Bible better/to speak in tongues so that I can pray more effectively. Please baptize me in the Holy Spirit now." Trust that as you pray according to God's will, He is working and answering your prayers.

Don't go through this life alone, on your own strength and ideas. Open your hands to the God who told you that you could ask Him for power, anointing, strength, and wisdom. Walk according to the Spirit, not the flesh. Don't abandon the wonderful gift of God's Holy Spirit in your life.

> *For John baptized with water, but you will be baptized with the Holy Spirit not many days from now.*
>
> —Acts 1:5

Final Principles

Jesus tells a story in Matthew 25 that we call "The Parable of the Talents." In short, Jesus talks about a man who is leaving on a long journey, so he leaves a sum of money with three of his servants. To the first he gives five talents, to the second he gives two, and to the last servant he gives one, instructing them to do business with it until he comes back. The first two go and invest their money and manage to double it. The third is afraid of losing it, so he buries it in the sand. The master comes back after some time and asks for an account from each of them. The first two are rewarded and given more responsibility and honor. The third is rebuked for being "wicked and lazy," and his one talent is given to the one who had ten. Then, Jesus says, "For to everyone who has, more will be given, and he will have abundance; but from him who does not have, even what he has will be taken away" (Matthew 25:29).

Jesus says this is what the kingdom of Heaven is like.

There are three things we need to learn from this story:

1. Even if you have less than everyone around you, what you have is significant.

A talent was approximately 15 years' wages. In today's currency, it would probably be around a million dollars, perhaps more. This is just to say that even though the last servant had "only" one talent, it was still quite a bit of money.

Though Jesus uses money as a metaphor, He is talking about something much greater than dollars and cents. God has given each of us "talents." He's given us each a package of assets that makes up a life: Your education, your experiences, your skills, your knowledge, your relationships, your resources, etc. Even the lowliest of us has been given quite a lot when we tally it all up.

Everyone has something great to offer to God.

2. God expects you to use what He has given you, to invest in His kingdom and reap returns.

In chapter 11 we talked about stewardship, the idea that all we have comes from God and we're really just managing it for Him. When our lives are over, God will want to know what we've done with His package of assets. He will want to know how we spent the time, resources, creativity, training, and opportunities that He has given us.

God opens doors, but doors don't stay open forever, and I'm sure you will agree that there is nothing more tragic than squandered opportunity. Most of us have potential but never enter into productivity, like a beautiful, sleek, powerful sports car that never gets on the road, never gets put on display. Ephesians 2:10 tells us, "We are His workmanship, created in Christ Jesus for good works, which God prepared beforehand so that we would walk in them."

What this means is that life is not all about fulfilling our shifting desires. Life is about pouring out our everything as an offering to God. It is about investing what we have to offer into His work.

Each of us has been given a different amount to invest. I like to think of my little espresso mug and my (much larger) cappuccino mug. They both hold coffee. One holds less, the other more. God doesn't expect an espresso mug to hold 16 ounces of coffee; He just expects it to be full, to be poured out, and to fill it up again. When that happens, something miraculous takes place: Growth. When we are faithful with what we've been given, just like in the story, more is given to us. We become a larger mug. This is not a "get rich quick" scheme or a ridiculous "manifest your money" seminar. This is Jesus' instruction on how we need to live, on how to usher in God's kingdom and reap spiritual blessings.

When we don't invest in God's kingdom or allow ourselves to be filled up by God and poured out on this world, we rust, we get cobwebs, and eventually our dusty, unused selves get put in the attic. What a tragedy. We are meant to be used.

This can look like many things, and I would caution you against succumbing to a guilty feeling of "I'm not doing enough." If you've just become a Christian, you probably are not going to become head pastor of a large congregation right away, for example. God knows how much capacity He has given us, and as we are faithful He will increase that capacity. We can't do everything, but we need to be doing something. Every day we ought to think and ask God, "Lord, what can I do with this package of assets that You have so graciously given to me? How can I use my personality, my freedom, my skills, my money, my time, etc. to bring Your kingdom to this world?"

We fulfill the Master's charge when we pour ourselves out on this world with God's love and when we learn His Word and commune with Him in prayer. We are to live by a different standard, to look different than the world around us, to imitate Jesus in every aspect of our lives, bringing His hope, truth, provision, and love to a hurting world. These things bring profit, and God's kingdom comes to a greater extent.

3. There is benefit to living this way.

The devil and our sinful flesh have promulgated a Ponzi scheme to us. We are constantly told, "If it feels good, do it. Spend your whole package of assets on yourself. In your marriage, just think about you. If it doesn't work out, find somebody else. At your job, just think about you. Ignore difficult people. Spend all of your money on entertainment and diversions." What is the end result? A nation with a skyrocketing suicide rate, crumbling families, a crisis of drug addiction, and increased division.

We've been putting sugar in the gas tank. God calls us to use the right fuel for our lives.

Jesus says in John 14:6 that He is the life. He tells us in John 10:10 that He came that we could have abundant life. God's way is the only way that works. It is the only way that satisfies. It is all that will give us purpose and meaning over the long haul.

God has given us each a great treasure, and we are to use it for His benefit. You have resources, you have a mind, you have His Word, and right here in this book you have 12 scriptures to memorize and apply to your life. God made you to accomplish good work. Don't let fear of failure or aversion to risk make you bury your gifts in the sand. Overcome the apathy and burn brightly for God. This is my final charge to you.

> *"Do not love the world nor the things in the world.... For all that is in the world, the lust of the flesh and the lust of the eyes and the boastful pride of life, is not from the Father, but is from the world. The world is passing away, and also its lusts; but the one who does the will of God lives forever."*
>
> —1 John 2:15–17

STUDY
GUIDE

WEEK 1

Chapters 0–2

CHAPTER 1: HOW TO TRUST GOD

1. Why do so many Christians struggle with trusting God? Can you think of a time when you struggled with this?

_____

_____

_____

_____

2. What are some examples of things people put their trust in rather than God?

_____

_____

_____

3. Pastor David said that if you trust God and His Word in decision-making, it will "set on fire the course of [your] life." What do you think he means by this statement?

_____

_____

_____

_____

4. What are some of the reasons you've heard Christians give for disobeying God?

_____

_____

_____

_____

5. If someone asked you why you trust God and His Word, what would you say?

_____

_____

_____

_____

_____

_____

CHAPTER 2: HOW TO BE FREE FROM THE PAST

1. Why do you think Jeremiah might have felt like a failure? Have you ever felt that way?

_____

_____

_____

_____

2. The life of Paul is a great encouragement to many. How does his life encourage you?

_____

_____

_____

_____

3. What was Paul's secret to moving ahead after a failure? In your life, have you found this easy to do?

_____

_____

_____

_____

4. For you personally, what is the best part of God's forgiveness?

_____

_____

_____

5. As a Christian, why is every day a new beginning? How could this impact your life?

_____

_____

_____

_____

_____

Week 2

Chapters 3–4

CHAPTER 3: HOW TO BE CONTENT

1. Is there an area of discontentment in your life? Is there something you don't have that you believe would make you happy? If so, what?

_____

_____

_____

2. What are the 3 steps to contentment?

_____

_____

_____

_____

3. Which step is hardest for you and why?

_____

_____

_____

_____

4. What does practicing have to do with contentment?

_____

_____

_____

_____

_____

CHAPTER 4: HOW TO WAIT

1. Why is waiting an inherent, inseparable part of God's promises?

_____

_____

_____

_____

2. When you wait on God, you position yourself to be _____.

3. Like King Saul, why do we panic in the midst of waiting? Why do we believe we have to help God out?

_____

_____

_____

_____

4. What are the 3 steps to waiting on God?

_____

_____

_____

_____

5. What is the one truth Pastor Dave hopes you remember from this chapter?

_____

_____

_____

_____

Week 3

Chapters 5–6

Chapter 5: How to Make Wise Decisions

1. What is biblical wisdom? How is it different from knowledge?

_____

_____

_____

_____

_____

2. What are the 3 ways to gain wisdom?

_____

_____

_____

_____

3. Why do we need to test what we think God may be saying to us?

_____

_____

_____

_____

_____

4. What is the eightfold test for determining whether or not God is actually speaking to you?

_____

_____

_____

_____

_____

_____

_____

_____

5. What does it mean to be double-minded in decision-making?

_____

_____

_____

CHAPTER 6: HOW TO PRAY

1. Why should we pray about everything?

_____

_____

_____

_____

2. Why can all of us have the faith to pray and, if need be (and in God's will), to even move a mountain?

_____

_____

_____

_____

3. How do we know if we are praying according to God's will?

_____

_____

_____

_____

4. What are God's 4 answers to our prayers?

_____

_____

_____

_____

_____

5. What would you say to someone who stopped going to church and following Jesus because God "never answered any of their prayers"?

_____

_____

_____

WEEK 4

Chapters 7–8

CHAPTER 7: HOW TO FIND STRENGTH IN WEAKNESS

1. How does pride keep people from coming to know Jesus as Lord?

_____

_____

_____

_____

2. Once we humble ourselves and see our need for a Savior, how can a haughty spirit limit our potential?

_____

_____

_____

_____

_____

3. Why is it good for a Christian to be in a place where he or she is admitting failures or inadequacies?

_____

_____

_____

4. Can you think of a time when pride kept you from letting God work through you?

_____

_____

_____

_____

CHAPTER 8: HOW TO LIVE WITHOUT WORRY

1. Why do so many people ultimately find themselves disillusioned and unhappy?

_____

_____

_____

_____

_____

_____

2. Define "being worried."

_____

_____

3. Why is worrying useless and counterproductive?

_____

_____

_____

_____

4. Why is it a good idea to do your devotions in the morning?

_____

_____

_____

_____

5. Why is 2 Corinthians 5:15 countercultural? Why are so many Christians miserable, confused, and depressed?

_____

_____

_____

_____

6. Why is it so important to take one day at a time?

_____

_____

_____

_____

_____

_____

WEEK 5

Chapters 9–10

CHAPTER 9: HOW TO ENDURE

1. What is the 4th Commandment?

_____

_____

2. What is the 1st purpose of the Sabbath? The 2nd?

_____

_____

_____

_____

_____

3. Why have Christians switched the Sabbath from Saturday to Sunday?

_____

_____

_____

_____

4. Failing to attend church regularly usually has consequences. What are they?

_____

_____

_____

_____

5. Why do we all need a weekly reminder of God's faithfulness?

_____

_____

_____

_____

6. Why does your church attendance matter?

_____

_____

_____

_____

_____

CHAPTER 10: HOW TO FEAR GOD

1. What helps to remind you of the awesomeness of God?

_____

_____

_____

_____

2. What is the basic definition of fearing God?

_____

_____

_____

_____

3. How would you explain to someone that fearing God is a good thing?

_____

_____

_____

_____

4. What is the most basic attribute of a Christian that fearing God helps with?

_____

_____

_____

_____

5. What are 2 keys to remember when thinking about fearing the Lord?

_____

_____

_____

_____

WEEK 6

Chapters 11–12

CHAPTER 11: HOW TO HONOR GOD WITH YOUR FINANCES

1. What did Jesus see in Zacchaeus that convinced Him that Zacchaeus had changed?

\
\
\
\

2. The Bible's teaching on money essentially boils down to 3 truths. What are they?

\
\
\
\

3. What are the 4 principles that the Prophet Malachi gives us in Malachi 3:7–12?

_____

_____

_____

_____

4. What are the 2 foundational truths to understand if you want to be a good steward?

_____

_____

_____

_____

5. Fill in the blank: Obedient, generous Christians reap _____ of God.

CHAPTER 12: HOW TO LIVE IN THE POWER OF GOD

1. How are the indwelling presence of the Holy Spirit and the Baptism of the Holy Spirit different?

_____

_____

_____

2. What are cessationists?

_____

_____

_____

3. Some people in the Church believe you must manifest this gift to authenticate being baptized in the Holy Spirit. What gift, and are they right?

_____

_____

4. How do you receive the Baptism of the Holy Spirit?

_____

_____

_____

5. What are some things that would keep Christians from asking to be baptized in the Holy Spirit?

_____

_____

_____

_____

NOTES